TRANSLATING
THE
TEENAGE ROAR

Understanding and Supporting Your Teen
With Transformative Ideas That Work

By Yaakov Rosenthal, CPLC, CSRT
With Shana Balkin

Manufactured in the United States of America.

ISBN: 9781797726045

Dedicated to my beloved parents, may they rest in peace, and to my support and my wife, Tzivia Chaya.

CONTENTS

Section I
The Adult's Role

Section II
Living New Possibilities

Section III
Handwriting Samples

Forward

THE WORLD WE LIVE IN has a lot of good to offer. Great strides are being continuously made in the realms of education, economic opportunity, technology, travel, health, wealth, and more. And yet, not everyone has altogether positive experiences. In my 19 years directing a Jewish school for teenagers who don't fit into the standard mold, it's become all too clear that there are always many, many people who struggle.

Some of these teens suffer real loss, or they have to deal with medical problems or other major issues. Some just don't feel they fit in anywhere; they haven't found their place. School isn't working for them. They're unsatisfied, not happy, not getting what they need. They feel lost, misplaced. And then there are those who have been mistreated, abused, or used, or who have very difficult home lives and relationships, leaving them with a strong distaste for life.

Even with all the real challenges and painful experiences so many teenagers go through, they're all simply expected to fit in somewhere and make it work. Yet we know it frequently doesn't exactly play out that way. On top of it all, there's often nobody who truly looks out for them.

Why do people endure pain, of any kind? Couldn't things happen differently? Why does it have to be like this? These are some of the greatest philosophical questions of life.

While I don't have the answers, I will say this:

The problem lies in seeing pain and struggle as negative. It's obvious that they are *experienced* as negative, but beneath that, they're really *neutral* packages filled with intense, immense energy waiting to be channeled in one direction or the other, for good or for bad.

Pain and struggle contain so much power that if we could somehow harness that power and transform the hurt into something constructive, it would produce incredible results.

History has proven that pain can stimulate tremendous change. Some of the greatest achievements mankind has ever known are the work of people who were cast aside, or who didn't make the cut, or who were handicapped, or who were considered failures, or crazy, or out of touch.

Here is a *very* partial list of dropouts, rebels, and failures who radically changed the world as we know it:

Susan B. Anthony	Benjamin Franklin
Clara Barton	Bill Gates
Ludwig van Beethoven	Helen Keller
Christopher Columbus	Abraham Lincoln
Michael Dell	Florence Nightingale
Emily Dickinson	Annie Oakley
Walt Disney	JK Rowling
Thomas Edison	The Wright brothers
Albert Einstein	Oprah Winfrey
Henry Ford	Mark Zuckerberg

Let's not forget that even the Bible has its fair share of characters who didn't fit the mold and yet changed the course of history: Abraham was an outcast and a rebel, yet he brought monotheism to the world. Joseph was sold out by his brothers and falsely imprisoned, yet he emerged as the viceroy of the world's most powerful kingdom, and his ideas kept vast parts of the planet (some opinions say the whole world!) from starvation in the face of a colossal famine. Moses was a wanted man, a fugitive with a pronounced speech impediment, yet he brought an entire nation out of slavery, through a sea, and into freedom. The list goes on.

The world needs people who struggle and even fail by the standard measures, forcing them to dig deeper and deeper, uncovering more and more energy, passion, creativity, and genius, to help the world take some great leaps it could never achieve otherwise.

I sent a lucky group of five teenagers from our school to a resort town in Mexico for the High Holidays this year. The local rabbi there needed assistance, and though he usually brought rabbinical students from the big New York yeshivahs to help him, this time it worked out for me to send our students.

The rabbi called me immediately after the holidays to put in reservations for a group from our school to come to him the following year. He no longer had any interest in the rabbinical students from New York. He said that, despite being a bit rough around the edges, our students were so real, so alive, so genuine, that he insisted they come back.

He's not the only one. Our school sent another group of nine to an army base near Buffalo, New York for Rosh Hashana. After the holiday, the rabbi there begged me to send an even bigger group for Yom Kippur, which I did. After that, he called me to insist we now make this a regular thing. Just to make a point here, he is inviting ten teenagers to his own home, where he has to feed them, take care of their needs, clean up afterwards, and pay for it all—and he insists we do this *as often as possible*. Our students have something special. The feedback I get is consistent: people have rarely seen this level of genuine caring, closeness, sincerity, or energy. Despite the often raw exterior—or perhaps because of it—the difference in our students opens people's eyes.

Our school was founded for this purpose. It's not just to help those who struggle—that they survive, overcome, and carry on with life—but rather to help them discover just how much greatness lies within their hearts, minds, and souls, just waiting to be uncovered and shared with us all. This job doesn't belong only to me as a school director—it's the job of every adult who interacts with struggling teenagers. The world needs what these young people have to offer. And it's up to us, the adults in their lives, to make it happen.

We don't always know what our teens are struggling with, nor do we always even know any struggle exists at all. But the reality is that all teenagers are struggling with *something*. Even for a typical teenager, the road can seem very dark. That's why it's so important for us to be their guiding light. Without attention, love, guidance, and care, even a seemingly small struggle left to fester can turn into tragedy. But a struggle in and of itself doesn't have to lead to something bad. From the most painful experiences can come the most beautiful things.

After working with Yaakov for more than a decade, I have witnessed time and time again the tremendous impact his skills, techniques, and method have had on countless students in our school and in many others. It is my confident expectation that this extraordinary book will provide you with a unique combination of tools and insights that will surely help you guide your teens through their inevitable struggles to the sweetest successes that can follow, with the right approach.

Rabbi Uri Perlman
Director and Founder of Bais Menachem Yeshiva
Wilkes-Barre, Pennsylvania

Note to Graphologists: You Can Do So Much (Less Is) More

WHEN SOMEONE GOES to a standard graphologist, he'll usually come away with a couple-page summary of one or two dozen of his own traits, several of which he needs to work on. He'll get all the little details, whether they really matter or not. Personally, I think that wastes time, especially the client's. That approach might be good for someone visiting a graphologist simply for the novelty of it, but not for someone who is truly seeking change or needs help. Such an abundance of information becomes overwhelming and thereby useless, nothing more than an exercise in me being a graphologist.

That's the thing; I don't see myself as a graphologist. I see myself as *using* graphology to get to the meat, as a vehicle to get into people's psyches. I want to help people create the change they crave and need in order to move forward with their lives. So instead of bombarding them with more information than they can handle or do anything with, I prefer to first focus on a few positive traits to build trust; then I choose one point, the lynchpin, the thing I think is really holding this person back. Once the person understands that basic concept, everything else will shift.

Through graphology, I teach people how to respect themselves, how judging is a false concept, how to invest in themselves, how to move on from the past. Graphology shows people that I know who they truly are, and it allows them to hear me, to *want* to hear me.

This, I believe with full conviction, is my responsibility as a graphologist. This work makes an impact. It changes lives. It changes relationships. I want to share and spread this approach, to inspire others to use graphology in this way.

If you are a graphologist, know that you have the potential to truly change people's lives, even faster and more powerfully than they could from months or years in therapy. I hope this book opens your eyes to your own potential, and to the tremendous impact you can have on a person's life.

Introduction

I N TEN MINUTES OR LESS, about 85 percent of teens I speak with trust me, open up to me, and are open to a new depth of understanding. This can take a therapist weeks or months, and many parents and educators don't accomplish it in a teen's lifetime.

There are three components to what I do in a meeting with a teenager:

1. Analyze the teenager's handwriting

When I look at a teen's handwriting sample, without having ever met him[1] before or even asking a single question, I can create a clear, multi-dimensional analysis of that teen's personality and experience. It's an incredible diagnostic tool for two reasons: The first is that as an adult, you can only truly be there for a teenager when you really know him and what's going on in his life. Graphology (handwriting analysis) gives you critical information that you might not have another way of getting.[2] The second reason is that once I *tell him* what I now know about him, he feels I "get" him, and he starts opening up and listening.

2. Listen to the teenager and allow him to feel understood

When he shares his experience, I listen without judgment and validate him. One of the main problems adults have with understanding teens

---

1   Though many general examples in this book will apply to both male and female teenagers and adults, I have chosen to use the pronoun "him" instead of "him/her" or "them" for the sake of better flow and ease of reading.

2   To be clear, I'm not suggesting you violate your teen's privacy; many teens actually find it interesting themselves and gladly give over a handwriting sample, an old piece of homework, etc.

is that the adults are constantly judging them without even realizing it. Teens unfairly have a bad rap just because they're teens. They often get little respect and a closed ear when they want to say something. (If this makes you feel defensive, that's understandable. But if you think about it honestly, I think you'll realize it's true.) When they see that I don't assume anything about them, that I am open to seeing them as they see themselves, that I listen, and that I accept them for who they are, they feel safe, and they want my advice.

3. Share insights from my 9 Principles for Living New Possibilities

These are culled from a number of sources in both neuroscience and Kabbalah and help teens learn to think practically, realistically, and without false worries.

These Principles are simple, but they're often new concepts for teens (and even many adults), who, thanks to the trust we've quickly developed, are now open to these ideas that can, and often do, radically change their lives.

Teens are notorious for not wanting to listen to anyone of authority, but time and time again, the teens I interact with want to know what I think, and they want to take my advice. Why? The combination of graphology, neuroscience, and Kabbalah is a veritable "dream team" of tools that gives me a tremendous understanding of what teens go through (individually and in general), how to relate to them, and how to communicate to them in a way that they actually *want* to listen.

Sometimes, the only way a teenager can express himself comes off as intimidating, off-putting, confusing, or even downright scary, like a lion roaring right in your face. Do you know why lions roar? It's not because they're mean. It's because that's how they know how to communicate. Yes, a roar can be intimidating. Yes, sometimes a roar means the lion wants to eat you alive. But a roar is not always a fearsome thing in and of itself. Sometimes a lion roars to locate other members of his pack, or to keep the peace between other lions, or to address something unusual in his environment. This book can help you translate your teenager's roar to a language you can understand and use effectively.

This book is *not* a textbook on graphology, neuroscience, or Kabbalah; it's more of a parent/teacher guide that's *informed by* graphology, neuroscience, and Kabbalah. While the graphology and neuroscience are included overtly in the book, the Kabbalah is more of an undertone woven throughout. It is the basis for my personal outlook on life, as well as the foundation for most of my 9 Principles for Living New Possibilities.

My purpose in writing this book is to offer you some information and tools that have worked so well for me in being able to connect with teens and make an impact on their lives, as well as to encourage you to have your teens' handwriting analyzed by a trained professional (or to have one regularly brought to your school if you're an educator).

I hope this book will show you that you don't have to be a therapist or a psychologist to help others. In fact, these techniques can have much more impact than therapy, and much faster. You as a parent or educator can make that impact without having to go through years and years of schooling.

This book can be read in sequence or randomly and offers parents and educators several things:

- Insight into the true workings of teens' brains
- Realistic ideas about what to expect from teens
- Important messages that need to be communicated to teens (and adults!) to maximize their self-esteem, their self-awareness, and

their awareness of the world around them, as well as to guide them during this crucial time in their lives

- A look into the tremendous insight of handwriting analysis

Unrealistic expectations for your teens causes them and you unnecessary stress, worry, confusion, and pain. So many parents and educators expect their teens to act and process information like adults, but they give them privileges and punishments as if they were children. It makes it nearly impossible for you to connect with them, or for them to connect with themselves.

On the other hand, realistic expectations coupled with clear communication, listening, and care fosters trust and closeness and allows teens to thrive.

This book is largely about helping teens sift through their insecurities, worries, and perspectives in a way that's honest, positive, and productive. However, it's important to note that many adults have insecurities, worries, and negative outlooks that can have a dramatic impact on their teens, as well, even into their teens' adulthoods. Know that a hurt teen left untreated becomes a hurt adult. Adults will need to do their own inner work, too, if they want the best shot of being there for their teens.

Luckily, it doesn't have to be all that complicated. Let's begin.

Do These Teens Sound Like Anyone You Know?

A 15-YEAR-OLD GIRL was asked to leave the school because the administration felt she was suicidal. They were worried that she would affect the other students. She claimed she was just looking for a reaction. P.S. No other school wants her.

An 18-year-old girl never gets into trouble. She gets good grades, and she's popular and responsible, but she worries she's not good enough. She's putting up a good front. She's depressed.

A 13-year-old boy is afraid he will never understand what life's all about. He gets good grades and stays out of trouble. He believes he will never be accepted.

A 16-year-old girl was flaunting her new boyfriend on Snapchat and Facebook. Four months later, she was involved in a threesome and an ugly break up. The school's response: If you play with fire, you'll get burned. She is angry and lost.

A 17-year-old girl has parents who are living their lives through her. She quietly suffers and wonders who *she* is.

A 15-year-old smiley boy just needs someone to talk to, but there is nobody available.

A 14-year-old boy's father is mentally ill. His mother has given up on being an involved parent. The boy went to foster care. He only trusts himself and his close friends.

Translating the Teenage Roar is a book about teens on their journey.

We often dismiss teens' experiences as overly dramatic, silly, or immature. We forget that these experiences *are their lives,* their whole reality. How we react will inform who they become as adults. Do you remember what it felt like to be a teenager? Your experiences mattered. Their experiences matter, too. Everyone wants to be happy, productive, and loved. These teens think they are small, insignificant, and not good enough. They need something to serve as the glue to put themselves together.

Section I

The Adult's Role

Chapter 1

Mythbusting: Teens Really Are Misunderstood

IT WAS ONCE BELIEVED THAT all significant human brain development was complete by age five. (This explains why so many parents try to jumpstart a young child's education with a tremendous amount of external stimuli.) For decades, there was little money in adolescent studies, and most funds went to researching either child development or aging. During the past 20 years, things have changed. In the early 2000s, with the increase of research money and the development of fMRI machines, researchers have discovered many significant differences between the brains of children, teenagers, and adults. **It is now accepted that the massive brain growth occurring between ages 12 and 24 is *on par* with brain development between birth and age five.** Wow!

Teenagers display behaviors unique only to them; they're not children, but they're not adults, either. The word "teenager" wasn't used until the 1940s when the age group started going to school instead of working, and it was determined a new name was needed for them.

There are many unfortunate myths surrounding teenagers. One myth says teenagers are racked with raging hormones. Newsflash: scientists have never identified a raging hormone! Yes, adolescents experience hormonal changes, but is there a clear link between these hormones and behavior? Because physical and behavioral changes start happening at the same time, it was assumed for more than a century that hormones must be responsible for both. **However, more recent studies show little to no correlation between hormones and adolescent behavioral changes.**

So if it's not all about the hormones, what is it?

We'll begin answering that question by introducing another myth, that teenagers are immature and just need to grow up. Yes, they do have a lot to learn, but the teen years are not a static state of being. We all have a lot to learn at any age. **And teens *are* learning, a lot, and fast.** To use an analogy by developmental psychologist Laurence Steinberg, this period of growth can be compared to "an accelerator without a brake." The "accelerator" is the limbic system, which controls feelings, pleasure seeking, and impulses. You could call it the emotional part of the brain. The "brake" is the prefrontal cortex of the brain, which controls things like planning, decision making, impulse control, social behavior, and expressions of individual personality. You could call it the rational part of the brain. These very different parts of the brain are developing at very different rates. The emotional part of the brain is present at birth and well developed by the time puberty hits, but the rational part of the brain develops much more slowly. Neither reaches full development until the early to mid twenties.

This means that **it's perfectly natural and *expected* for a teenager to take dangerous risks, choose pleasure over practicality, do strange things in public, and act dramatically** about things that wouldn't ruffle your feathers at all. It also means that **it's normal for teenagers to be confused about their personal identities and to experiment with different personas**, because their brains are physically and chemically in "Who Am I?" mode, working diligently to figure out their personalities.

Before age twelve, a child is usually the center of his environment, and everything else is secondary. There's no thought of individual identity because that requires differentiation from *others*, and they're not *aware* of others. For the child, everything he experiences revolves around his needs, his wants, and his happiness or discomfort. Only once children become aware of the outside world can they start to wonder who they really are and how they're different from (or similar to) others. As the dawn of the teenage years arises, suddenly they realize the world is a lot bigger than they'd realized. Now they are abruptly forced to ponder, where's my place? What's my connection? What do I think of all this? What does everyone else think of *me*? Everyone tells teens not to judge others, but what does that mean when it appears that everyone judges everyone else constantly? The whole focus of their awareness shifts. There are so many new ideas to navigate. There are school responsibilities, home and family obligations, social expectations, and countless other new situations. On top of all that, teens are handling many, many, many mistakes.

This brings me back to the previous question, "so if it's not all about the hormones, what is it?" **It's about underdeveloped cognitive abilities.** We blame their irrational and dramatic behavior on hormones when really it's due to the fact that they literally haven't learned to think straight and are being faced with new experiences for which they have zero frame of reference. This is an important distinction because "the hormone problem" implies that teens are hopeless until their hormones even out, but "the thinking problem" means that they can be taught. It's important to note that I'm not blaming any adult for assuming that making effort with teens is a lost cause; we've been conditioned both by their behavior and by societal norms to see them that way. But in reality, teens are a far cry from a lost cause.

It's the same issue with saying that "teenagers are immature and just need to grow up." It's a clutch, another excuse to not make adequate effort with teens. In reality, they're going through changes that are *truly* dramatic and challenging. Do these challenges make teens incapable until they grow up? Of course not! They're capable, but they're learning. It's not easy. And just like any of us needs support during our most confusing and difficult times, **teenagers desperately need to feel supported and loved unconditionally now maybe more than ever.** Their desire to explore, test boundaries, and experience the unknown will set the tone for their adult lives. They need to be educated, guided, and loved, not merely tolerated, punished, or dismissed.

They need to know that you'll stand by them during their scariest, loneliest, least glamorous moments, that you'll be there for them when they fail, and that you won't judge them for their mistakes.

Next myth: teenagers need to move from being dependent in their world to being independent. First of all, no one is truly independent; rather, we are all interdependent. We rely on each other for basic needs like food, clothing, and electricity, as well as more complex needs like attachment, love, and family. Both teens and adults need to realize this. Teens rely on adults, and on each other. Adults also rely on their teens. We *all* need each other.

The next myth is that teens are physically resilient and can do little damage to their bodies during these years. This is especially pertinent to teenage drinking and drug use. The idea that teens can rebound from any destructive behavior without any permanent damage could not be further from the truth. As a child enters the teenage years, just like in infancy, the brain is ready to be customized. The actions that the teen performs are what customizes the brain. These years can be spent learning to play a musical instrument or to scroll through pictures on Instagram, to shoot a basketball or to steal, to dance or to abuse alcohol and drugs. There are studies showing that teen marijuana use causes permanent brain damage, and that teenage drinking is linked to a number of serious long-term health issues. Not only that, but abuse of drugs and alcohol in teen years can set the tone for addictive and dangerous behaviors for the rest of their lives.

Not just regarding drugs and alcohol, but all a teenager's experiences, for better or for worse, will mold the teenager into the adult he'll one day become.

It would be absurd to expect a five-year-old to pick up a hundred-pound weight. The young child has not developed—nor is he even capable of developing—that kind of strength at that age. It would be even more absurd to criticize or punish the child for his lacking strength. Similarly, most teenagers have not developed the cognitive ability to control their emotional desires and curiosities with reason and logic. On the other side of the spectrum, it would also be absurd to think a five-year-old couldn't learn to spell his own name. He could if given proper guidance. So too, we owe it to our teens not to expect too little of them.

After all of these myths are debunked, we see very clearly how thoughtful and deliberate we must be with our expectations from our teenagers. It's a very fine balance between understanding their strengths and limitations, setting boundaries, giving some freedom, and trusting them to make as many good choices as they can with the tools they have. It's also about holding them *appropriately* accountable for their actions, and showing them support no matter how many times they fail. This period is a real balancing act between nature and nurture. There's much that's left up to their changing bodies and to chance, but there's much that's left up to them, and perhaps even more left up to us, the adults in their lives.

OCT 6, 2014 10:27 PM

POSTED BY ANONYMOUS

I'm sick of my parents not understanding me!

I'm not perfect, I'm not my older sister either.

I don't get on well with other girls and yes! Most of my friends are older boys.

GET OVER IT!!!

I am who I am and I just wish they would understand that.

My Mum doesn't stop trying to make me into a mini version of her or my older sister.

I'm sick of being judged by everyone because of my family and having them all automatically assume I'm perfect.

I'm my own person... Stop trying to change me

In saying all of this I do know that my parents love me to pieces and would do absolutely anything for me. I also know they're just doing their best to make me into a good, responsible person.

I guess being a teenager is just frustrating.

SEP 12, 2014 10:07 AM

POSTED BY ANONYMOUS

Im a 14 year old and I can absolutely relate to the above article. My parents disapprove of any form of social media and it drove me insane. I finally opened a facebook & twitter account without them knowing and it got discovered. We fought and are not on good speaking terms. They dont approve of me meeting my friends outside of school and that hurts me a lot. I feel like Im under house arrest all the time. And whenever I ask them about their past they told me all these stories about being perfect and it drives me crazy. They also sometimes compare me to my brother and some of they're friends kids. It hurts me a lot thinking they cant accept my indivduality. They dont particulary like the clothes i wear, the music I listen to, the make up I prefer, or the fact that I depend on my friends approval to boost my self esteem. I never propery appreciate me for the good grades I get and when I get a bad onethey shout at me and give me a lecture that kills my self esteem. I wish they understood

DEC 29, 2013 05:22 PM

POSTED BY ANONYMOUS

I have the same problem like this. I just don't feel independent, if you know what I mean. Me and my parents have fights almost EVERY day because of this! The computer and social media helps me to express my feelings more than to keep them closed. I sometimes have the feeling of committing suicide which leads to my life full of lies. I do what I like best, and my parents think that I would get stalked or possibly kidnapped by the time I socialize online with people I don't know. Even if I don't know them, look into that fact more. I talk with people around my age group in virtual world games. They help me! My parents? THEY GROUND ME. I feel like I just want to live in the world I know online, not reality. My parents even put "Splashtop Streamer" to see what the heck I am doing. I don't care. I just want them to understand me more. Roleplay, they have no clue what it means. I roleplay and talk with those who have the same interests as me. My mobile devices got taken away cuz of this....

NOV 9, 2013 11:52 PM

POSTED BY ANONYMOUS

I am 14 and I really wish my parents knew that I HATE HATE HATE it when hey give me the infamous "when I was your age" lecture. It immediately shuts me off. I either sit there and zone out, or think to myself "kill me now…" I wish they would get that I know they weren't perfect when they were teens. They're not fooling anyone! Problem is, we get that, but it's wag more important that they get it too. I have all GT (gifted and talented) classes, and they never say anything about that. When I get a good grade in an exam, they say, "that's very nice." And when I don't, they say "You never get good grades" and the , they talk about how perfect they were when they were 14 year olds. Come on! I can tell that I am smarter than when they were in ninth grade, but they don't seem to get it! I wish I have the guts to say that to them, but my parents (hopefully not like yours) do the worst job of understanding! :'(

NOV 4, 2013 12:33 PM

POSTED BY ANONYMOUS

I am a 20 year old and all I really wish for was that my parents would thank my more when I do them a favour make supper clean the house and abide there rules . I am 20 years old I earn my own well hard worked for salary I pay rent and everything I may need even if I wanted a chocolate my parents would not even give me a penny whilest they have all the money they spend on others why can't they ever have time for me and expect me home by 9 in the week which by the way I'm only alouwed out once a week over weekends I have to be home by 11 I can't do anything its driving me insaid but what's huring me the very most is that they will not once say they proud of me and when I'm @ work or any where everyone goes on about what a great child I am I work so hard I have always I got head girl of sport in high school was top in almost everything I did and I have got great promotions which woman working in the company wanted and I got it out of everyone I was chosen I was noticed they never ask [anything.]

Dear Mr. Rosenthal,

My first thoughts were is this really going to help me? Am I going to be able to change? Not only did I completely change, but Mr. Rosenthal also taught me how to believe in myself.

There are times when I'm feeling doubtful about myself. He helped me put my thoughts into words and make it clear what I have to fix. All along, I did not know how I would ever improve. I spoke to people but gave up.

When I heard Mr. Rosenthal was coming to my school, I knew he would tell the truth and I was afraid to hear it. When we had our first session, everything he said made so much sense, and I felt so free.

He inspired me to work on myself right away. I put my whole self into it.

In one of the last sessions, I heard the words, "You did it! You became a happy and confident person." And, "Keep going."

From these words, I knew I have the potential to move higher, with thanks to Mr. Rosenthal.

MK, age 15

CHAPTER 2

What Impact Are You Having?

YOU *WILL* HAVE AN IMPACT on your teens no matter what you do. The question is, will the impact be positive...or negative?

Nature is *not* responsible for the all too common reality of teenagers shutting out adults—nurture is. Because so few adults know how to effectively interact with teens, **teens learn that adults are not to be trusted.** This can be dangerous on many levels. It doesn't have to be this way.

You can have positive, dramatic, lasting impact on your teens without having to go through years of schooling. You don't have to be a therapist or guidance counselor to connect with your teen; in fact, my techniques can be far more effective than months or years in therapy.

The teenage years bring person's very first opportunity to learn about himself and the world around him from a place of independence. As discussed earlier, the emotional part of the teen brain is far more developed than the reasoning part of the brain, so teens are not fully capable of understanding their choices. The plentiful mistakes they will surely make are ripe for positive learning opportunities, as well as a powerful potential for close relationships with older, wiser adults who can serve as loving role models and sources of support. But all too often, the adults unwittingly forfeit their opportunities for those close relationships by punishing or criticizing their teens for their mistakes and offering no understanding. Instead of learning how not to repeat the mistake, unfair punishments teach teens to just avoid the adult and even likely *repeat* the mistake, sometimes just out of hurt and spite. ("I'll show *him*!") Since the adults in their lives have betrayed them, now they only trust themselves and other teens.

The obvious problem is that they *aren't* experienced or logical enough to safely rely on themselves alone. They *do* need adults to help provide reason, experience, and strength for the things they don't yet know from their own experience or logic. This is why it's so important for adults to establish trust, to make teens feel safe to be who they are, with all their flaws. **They need to know that it's safe to make honest mistakes, and that it's safe to come to the adults who can help guide them.**

By the way, I'm not just talking about "problem kids." Even teens with seemingly no issues still need attention and guidance. Everyone is going through something. It's not infrequent that the "good kids" who got no special attention when they were teenagers wind up with issues in adulthood that could have been avoided with minimal support during their teenage years. Even just small talk about the seemingly mundane things in their day can have a major effect. This is a large part of what I do with my time when schools hire me to counsel their students. So often we just talk about the little things. Even this is powerful. They feel heard and understood, and they learn that some adults *can* be trusted not to judge or punish them.

This does not mean that teenagers shouldn't be responsible for their actions; it means they should face *appropriate*, logical consequences, without any unnecessary harshness or judgment. For example, if a teenager speeds on the highway and subsequently wrecks your car, he doesn't need to be screamed at or lectured for you to make your point. First of all, he's probably already scared and upset and needs comfort. He will still learn his lesson if you simply give him a hug, ask if he's okay, and tell him you're relieved he's not hurt, then revoke his car privileges until you feel he's ready and have him pay off the repair expenses and rental car for the interim. He will see that you do expect him to take responsibility for himself, but also that you love him, and that you're not judging him for making a pretty normal mistake. Remember, even adults make stupid mistakes, and unwise risk taking is *biologically wired in every single teenager.* **You can demand accountability *and* offer love and understanding at the same time,** without expecting more of them than their *bodies* are capable of. If you scream at him and tell him how irresponsible he is and ask how he could be so thoughtless, he will feel attacked for making an easy, albeit scary, mistake. He will learn that you don't get it, that you don't have his back, that you're judgemental, and that there's no point in talking to you, even at a time when he is scared, upset, and needing support. Then when he's in trouble and needs help, you won't be the person he turns to, and the person he *does* turn to might not be qualified for the job.

Imagine your fifteen-year-old gives in and drinks too much at a party, and now the party is over. He knows it's not safe to drink and drive. All of his friends were drinking, too. The only way he can think of to get home safely is to call you to pick him up. In the past, you've lectured and yelled at him for all his mistakes. Do you think he'll call you, or will he avoid getting judged and yelled at and let a drunk friend drive him home instead? I'll say it again: unwise risk taking is biologically wired in every single teenager. If he doesn't trust you, it is extremely likely he'd reason that he'll probably be fine and that drunk driving is worth the risk if it means avoiding criticism and punishment. On the other hand, if you've always shown him you support him despite his mistakes and never judge him, he might not be too scared to ask you for help.

Mr. Rosenthal is really superb looking into the real you. He described clearly my personality and character traits. He put into personal terms things in my life that I probably would not have contemplated or dealt with. After being analyzed four times from the beginning of this year, I can see how much I've grown and matured. He was a great help in this.

I thank Mr. Rosenthal for everything he brought to my attention and for his good advice.

Thank you,
MN, age 17

CHAPTER 3

Empathy, Acceptance, and Understanding: Non-Negotiable Prerequisites to Teaching

Their Perspective Is the Key to Teaching Yours

I't's easy to get caught up in the idea that we, the adults, have more knowledge, experience, and ability to reason, and that therefore we are the only ones with a right to our perspectives. The problem is that our being right doesn't change the way they feel or see things.

Try lecturing a two-year-old that it's irrational to throw a fit about not being allowed to play catch with your butcher knife. He hears you say it's not safe, but what does that even mean? Has he ever *seen* anyone get hurt with that knife? As far as he knows, it's shiny, it's big, it's cool, and he wants it. No matter how right you are, that doesn't change the fact that his perspective is real *to him*. It needs to be respected. Does that mean you should let him play with knives? No! It means that, **even when enforcing your rules based on your knowledge and experience, you still need to honor his feelings if you expect positive results.**

By the way, are we *always* right just because we're adults? Obviously not. I'm sure you know plenty of adults who are wrong plenty of the time. Our teens are right much more than we might think, but how often do we really give them the chance to share their side? How often are we really open to truly listening, to sincerely considering the possibility that they're right, that we'd have done the same thing if we'd been in their shoes?

A mom recently told me her daughter had dropped her smartphone and broken it. The mom calmly took a few minutes to ask her daughter why that had happened and what she could do in the future to prevent this kind of thing. Had she been messing around? Could she have been more careful? Was she not paying attention? The daughter responded to her, "Mom, I'm only human." This mom stopped and thought for a moment. Her response: "You're right. You're only human. I'm human too, and I also make mistakes. I'm sorry."

She could have reprimanded her daughter or lectured her about being careful with expensive things. She could have assumed that her daughter must have been doing something wrong. The reality is that responsible adults break phones every single day. Mistakes happen. Not everything needs to be an overt lesson in doing a better job next time. This mom took the opportunity to teach one of the most invaluable things possible: that she "gets" it. She took a situation that could easily have pushed her daughter away by making her feel that she had unfair standards, and instead, she reinforced their relationship with understanding, sincerity, and trust.

Let's take a different example. (Although the child in the story is not quite a teenager yet—around 11 years old at the time—the point is still just as relevant for any age.) I recently visited some friends who are genuinely good people and loving parents. They are very deliberate about the way they interact with their children, and all the kids are pretty happy and healthy, but the mother had shared with me that she'd been struggling a bit with one of their daughters, let's call her Lilly. That afternoon when we were visiting them, Lilly had been playing with some other neighborhood kids. All of a sudden, Lilly stormed into the kitchen where her mom and I were chatting. Lilly was visibly upset. Even physically, you could tell she was worked up; she was red in the face, breathing heavily, and sweating up a storm.

"Sara is so mean, Mommy!" the daughter said. "She hates me!"

"She doesn't hate you," her mom replied, "why would she invite you to play if she hated you?"

"She was *so* mean, and she was only mean to me."

"I really don't think she hates you," the mom said calmly as she continued chopping vegetables, "I think she has some social problems and doesn't really understand how to interact with other kids."

"No, that's not it," the daughter replied with even more frustration. "She *really does* hate me. She does." The daughter left the kitchen with a *harumph*, shoulders slumped, eyebrows furrowed, and mouth closed tightly.

Why hadn't she taken any comfort in her mother's words? Despite good intentions, my friend had denied Lilly's perspective, essentially telling Lilly her feelings were wrong. This didn't help Lilly; instead, she left feeling frustrated, misunderstood, and probably pretty helpless.

It's very possible that Lilly's friend really did just have social issues and really didn't hate her at all. But Lilly's experience was still very real *to her*. From Lilly's perspective, her mom was denying the facts and was totally out of touch with reality. In other words, Lilly's mom just didn't get it.

Do you think Lilly will be more likely or less likely to come to her mom the next time she experiences something upsetting? Could situations like these have something to do with why my friend was struggling with Lilly in general?

There is a time and a place for parents to share their perspective if they want to be heard. **The teen needs and deserves to be validated first.** For example, imagine if this story had gone a little differently.

"Sara is so mean, Mommy!" the daughter said. "She hates me!"

"What happened?" her mom asked her, "that sounds awful."

"She was nice to everyone but me."

"Wow, it sounds like she really hurt your feelings."

"Yeah."

"I used to have friends like that, too. It didn't feel good. If she doesn't like you, why do you think she invited you over?"

"I dunno."

"Would you like to hear what I think?"

"OK."

"Well, everyone is good at some things and not as good at other things. Like for example, I'm good at cooking, but I'm not so good at math. So, some kids are not so good at interacting with other kids, even when they like them. I wonder if Lilly might be like that, and even when she likes someone, she sometimes acts like she doesn't. Do you think that's possible?"

"I dunno. Maybe."

"She might not even realize she's acting mean. She does keep inviting you over, after all. But either way, it's no fun to be around someone when they're acting like that. I'm sorry she hurt your feelings."

When you deny a teen's reality, you make him feel that you don't understand (or don't care) what he's going through. When he doesn't feel you understand what he's going through, he might try to show you for a while, but he'll quickly learn there's no use in talking to you. But. If you first show him you get what he's going through, that you know it's hard, that you understand why he feels that way, and that you would feel the same way if you two switched places, he will first see that you actually do understand. He now has a reason to listen to you and to consider your ideas.

Imagine you go to the doctor for a sore throat. You walk into the doctor's office, and before you even get a chance to tell him what's wrong, he tells you he's going to need to amputate your foot. *What?!* He hasn't examined you or even spoken to you! Why on earth would he decide that, and why on earth would you listen?

This is an extreme example, but we do the same thing every single day with our teenagers. **We react to things and make decisions without ever hearing them out.**

When kids don't feel like their parents "get" them, they're not so likely to confide in them, and they're not so likely to take their parents' advice. Would you heed someone's personal advice if that person didn't really know you?

You can only truly be there for your teen when you are actually able to understand what's going on with him, and you can't possibly understand what's going on with him if you don't take the time to really truly listen to him without an agenda. The listening has to be for the sole purpose of listening and understanding. If you're listening in order to better make *your* point, or just nodding and saying *uh huh* until it's your turn, you've defeated the purpose. Aside from the fact that you'll have gained no insight about the inner workings of your teen's world, he will sense it, and you will only be resented.

Even when you are absolutely positive that you already know everything you need to know about a situation, you might very possibly *still* be wrong. How many times have you tried to explain something to someone who refused to consider your perspective but would have had a totally different understanding if he'd just listened? As Bill Nye (yup, that Bill Nye) so wisely put it, "Everyone you will ever meet knows something you don't." Even your kids!

If we want teens to listen, we need to make it clear that it's worth it to them. We have to show them that we consider their experience and perspective, and, within ourselves, we also have to consider their capacity for understanding. This truth needs to be as obvious to us with our teenagers as it is with our toddlers. Listen to them. Really hear their ideas. Speak gently and calmly. **Be someone your teens want to listen to.** Be someone they can trust.

The only chance of a teen really caring and wanting to listen to what you have to say is if you have your teen's trust and respect. If things with your teen have been rocky until now, it can take time, patience, practice, and consistency of really being there for your teen before you can expect your teen to start responding to you differently. You might notice a change right away, but you might not. Don't rush it. Don't give up. Nothing in the world is more worth waiting for.

Don't Be a Predator

Parents are often predators. I'm not talking about abusive parents; I'm talking about all parents, even great parents.

Um, excuse me?

The human body is programmed to protect itself. When it feels threatened, the brain's higher-level thinking shuts off and puts all its energy into physically protecting the self. This is a basic instinct that helps the body function at maximum capacity when it needs to, for example, run from a predator. If the brain were spending its energy thinking about the threat, it might not have the time to survive. "Hmm...that bear is getting closer...it looks scary...should I run? Maybe I'm misreading things?" So instead, it just kicks into gear and runs away. This instinct is enabled not just for threats of life and limb; it's anytime a person feels threatened by anything. *A person cannot think straight when he feels threatened.*

It might not seem the same as being attacked by a bear, but criticism, nagging, yelling, and sometimes even just asking a question are processed in the brain exactly like an attack. The thinking part of the brain shuts down, and the person will do anything to protect himself, even if it doesn't seem logical. **As far as the brain is concerned, when you criticize, you become a predator.** It's you against him. Even if your message is an important one, and even if you feel like you're coming from a loving place, it will not get through. This isn't just an annoying character trait about some people; it's a scientific fact about all humankind.

But that's life; sometimes something uncomfortable or undesirable has to be said. So how can it be done without pushing the teen away? By showing him *first* that he's safe. *First*, he needs to know that it's not you against him, that you're in this *with* him, that you're not judging him, that you get it, that you support him, that you don't hold anything against him.

Then, and only then, can you communicate ideas that would otherwise seem threatening, in a way that they can grasp them and want to make changes.

This means that they need to have an overall feeling and experience of safety/non-judgment from you, but also that *in that moment* they need to be shown that you're in this together, that it's *not* you against them.

So much of our energy is spent making sure we can trust our teens, but **how often do we do what it takes to make sure *they* can trust *us?*** Do you remember being a kid? Do you remember being reprimanded harshly for something you felt was completely unfair? Do you remember being "taught a lesson" and feeling like your parents had no clue what they were talking about? Did you ever feel like your friends were the only people who *really* got you? Why do we forget these feelings when *we* become parents? Why do we forget to pay attention to our kids' perspectives?

I have seen countless teenagers make major life changes after having their handwriting analyzed and learning my 9 Principles for Living New Possibilities. But the only way they're open to what I have to say is by showing them that I understand them and that I don't judge them. If either piece is off, everything I say will fall on deaf ears.

Teens need someone to understand them, not fix them.

The Love Part

Most of us didn't get into the parenting or teaching business because we just have so much information we want to tell someone smaller than us. We got into it because of love. We got into it because we value close connections. Because we love children. But it's easy to lose the forest for the trees.

A parent's power lies in listening to his teen, but that's also the key to a loving relationship between them. In the midst of all the mental energy that it takes to keep teens alive (joking...sort of), we often forget about fostering a close relationship with them. Sometimes, by the time we remember, it's too late.

Let's revisit the "fight or flight" thing, how people instinctively turn off their rational brains when they are criticized or nagged. Remember that this instinct is a reaction to the presence of a *predator*. Now how likely does it seem that a teenager (or any person, for that matter) would feel a close connection to someone his brain views as his predator? Not very. On that same note, it's not possible to develop a healthy bond with someone who doesn't feel listened to, because someone who doesn't feel listened to doesn't feel cared about.

How are our children going to grow up with a healthy self-image if their parents (and educators) don't listen to them or value their thoughts and opinions? The home is the number one place where children learn their own value. If their parents don't value their thoughts, feelings, and opinions, it's very likely they will grow up believing their thoughts, feelings, and opinions don't matter. And if their thoughts, feelings, and opinions don't matter, how could they believe that *they* matter at all? **If your own parents do not seem to accept you, that must mean you're unacceptable, right?** These issues can run deep and often last a lifetime.

This is a recipe for disaster for so many reasons. Firstly, as mentioned earlier, it will lead them to think, "Why should I listen to them when they have no idea what's going on with me?" And to a large extent, they'll be right! But more importantly, it keeps them from feeling you accept them. If you don't accept your teen, don't expect him to have a healthy self-esteem or self-image. All anyone wants is to know that they are good enough just the way they are. Accepting someone the way he is does *not* mean there isn't room for growth; in fact, growth is much more likely for a person who feels accepted as he is. Acceptance is a true human need. A teenager (or any person) who isn't finding that acceptance at home will go seeking it elsewhere, and you won't be the one to decide where your teen turns. It could be in dangerous places.

On top of that, the way a person is treated at home is often the way he learns to treat others. How do you want your teenager to learn to treat his classmates, and you, and one day his spouse and children? Do you want him to honor their perspectives, tolerate their mistakes with patience and understanding, show them without a doubt that he will always support and cherish them...or do you want him to have unreachable expectations, think his opinion is the only one that matters, and have a short fuse?

A teenager with parents who show him that they value his thoughts and feelings, want to know his experience, and can be trusted not to judge him for being a normal teenager and person; who react calmly, gently, and with understanding to challenges and aren't scary to be around; who remember what it was like to be a teenager and treat their teen the way *they* would want to be treated—a teenager with parents like these is much more likely to both respect and feel attached to his parents, to love and respect himself and make good choices, and to treat others with care and respect, too.

It is important to note that many teens are not seeking out a change in their lives. But a show of faith and encouragement from parents and teachers can inspire a dramatic change of direction and even personality, transforming the teenager's life for the better, even if the teenager isn't looking for it. The power of outside support cannot be overstated.

The Value of Empathy: One Parent's Perspective

Hi Yaakov,

I wanted to email you after our recent conversation about parenting and empathy to share some other thoughts about how critical empathy and listening are. I get the sense that many parents and teachers struggle with understanding how they solve anything.

I want to mention that it's not only about the individual situations that occur, it is about how this person, this child, learns to feel about himself or herself and develop into an adult. I'm almost 40. I was definitely not raised with a lot of empathy or understanding. My parents were very loving in the ways that they knew how to be, they were and are really good people who wanted to do good by us. But they were extremely authoritative, obedience was the most important thing above all else, there was always a lot of pressure on me, and I felt very much that my feelings never mattered. Sometimes I would try to share my feelings, but it was never met with understanding.

That's not to say they didn't care, but I was either always asked why the thing I was upset about happened, what can I do to fix it, etc. It was as if I was to blame for my feelings, that the feelings themselves were unimportant, and taking care of the problem was all that mattered. Feeling that my feelings didn't matter in turn made me feel that I didn't matter to them, because if you love somebody, wouldn't you care if their feelings are hurt? And when the people who are supposed to know you and love you the most in the world make you feel like you don't matter, it doesn't make for a very healthy self-image. While I excelled in school, and on the outside seemed to be doing great, I had very low self-esteem, a lot of anxiety, fear of my parents, a feeling that they didn't know me or understand me or **want** *to know me, and to be honest, while we have worked through some of this as adults, I still feel that way about them to a large degree, and even feel afraid when I see my parents' names on the caller ID.* **I'm an adult. I shouldn't feel that way anymore. But I do.**

I feel that it's also important to mention that feeling like I don't matter, in other words, feeling worthless, can lead to a lot of really bad, even life threatening, decisions. For years I only dated jerks and losers who treated me like dirt because I felt like I didn't deserve any better and I was being treated so poorly because surely I had done something wrong and if only I would fix what I had done surely they're going to like me more, be more respectful, treat me with dignity, etc. I literally could have easily died in some of the situations I got myself into with men, and that was a direct result of feeling like I didn't matter. I am very lucky and blessed that I eventually learned that I do matter and should be treated with respect, even if I don't feel that way inside, and I found a husband who treats me that way, but many people are not so lucky, and get themselves into abusive relationships, and all sorts of awful things because of feeling the way I felt and still feel every day.

Now, not only with my parents, but with my husband, with friends, all over my life, I have a really hard time feeling like I matter, like people really like me, even when they do care. It's a complex I have now. I have social anxiety, anxiety in general, depression, an eating disorder, a fear of doing things even when I know I'm good at those things and would succeed, a lot of residual emotional issues that I wonder if I would have today had I been told, explicitly or implicitly, that the way I felt was important.

And the hard part is that even though I have the intellectual awareness of where my current issues come from, it's very hard to fix those things as an adult. *You can't just erase your past. You can work through it, and I believe and hope that I will feel confident and good one day, but I'm many years into the process, the therapy, the self-help books, the support groups, sometimes medicine, lots of things, and I'm still nowhere near being the confident, healthy person that I want to be. Not to mention, I didn't get to have the carefree happy-go-lucky fun childhood that every child deserves.*

…And remember, I come from a family with stable parents who loved me very much and really truly tried to do their absolute very best at every moment, and this still happened *because of a heavy focus on obedience and problem-solving, and because no one ever made me feel that my feelings were important. I'm not saying ALL my problems today are my parents' fault, as I'm sure there are other factors at play, but I do believe their role was major.*

*I'm sharing this because **I'm not sure people realize how devastating it can be for a person's life long-term if they don't get that empathy piece.** And while I feel a little embarrassed to share this stuff about myself, I feel like if I can help other parents and teachers, who obviously love and want to be there for their kids just like my parents did, avoid having their kids turn into adults who feel like I do, it's worth it to share it.*

GT, age 39

CHAPTER 4

Common Downfalls In Adult-Teen Interactions

Overparenting

OVERPARENTING OFTEN LEADS TEENS to have a poor sense of self, lacking problem-solving skills, and little resilience in the face of challenges. Teens need some room to live their own lives. Sometimes a parent will need to put his foot down, but if feet were meant to *always* be down, they'd have been planted in the ground. Give your teens the opportunity to feel some autonomy, make some mistakes, and learn from them, with your support and guidance behind them.

Being Too Strict

Though many parents feel that being extra strict will make sure their kids are kept in line, studies show that it actually makes them more likely to rebel. When teens feel their parents inhibit them from having fun or making their own choices, they lose respect for their parents. It can even make them lose respect for authority in general, and it can cause them to lash out in seriously dangerous ways (think crime, addiction, etc.).

Yelling

A University of Pittsburgh study showed that, as far as a kid's emotional health is concerned, there's no difference between yelling and hitting or spanking. Not only can parental yelling lead to children having aggression and social issues, but the study also showed that yelling doesn't even get kids to have better behavior. It actually accomplishes the opposite, causing kids to misbehave more.

Nagging

Researchers at at Harvard and Universities of Pittsburgh and California-Berkely found that critical parts of the brain turn off when the person is being criticized, making it difficult, if not impossible, to even understand the information being communicated.

Hypocrisy

Parents often feel that they have a parental right to break their own rules. A mother tells her son not to yell, but then she yells at him. The problem is that teens pick up on every little thing you do, whether you like it or not. Every adult the teen sees, even if it's just in line at the grocery store, is contributing to his ever-developing definition of what an adult is, and how adults act. Obviously, parents and teachers usually have the greatest effect since the more time the teen spends with the adult, and the more intimately the adult is involved in the teen's life, the more the adult's actions will affect him. This will determine his feelings on whether adults can be trusted in the present, but it will also determine what he thinks is appropriate and expected for *his* future as an adult. No matter what lessons adults preach, nothing will last like the images of what he sees adults actually *do*.

Bequeathing Your Baggage to Your Teens

We all had lives before our children were born. Most of us have endured pain of some kind. Some of us have had truly traumatic experiences that still live with us, or have mental health conditions that impede us from feeling our best, or have difficult challenges in our jobs, marriages, or any other part of our lives. We are all humans who experience difficulty. Sometimes, without our meaning to, our children become the brunt of our own personal issues that really don't have anything to do with them.

It is a natural part of the human condition that sometimes two human beings will cause each other pain, but it's our responsibility to do as little of that as possible to our vulnerable children who are looking to us for love, guidance, answers, and validation. **It is imperative that we work on our own problems.** There is a Jewish saying that implores us to "love your fellow as you love yourself." One classic interpretation of this saying is that a person can *only* love another person as much as he loves himself. And while many of us would argue that we love our children or spouses far more than we love ourselves, it's not just about what we feel for the other person. It's about how that love is expressed...or isn't. **If you love your child more than anything else in the world, but you're too broken from your own problems to be there for him, he doesn't benefit from that love.** Part of loving our children is making sure that we are our best selves so that all the love we have for them can be expressed in the healthiest, truest way possible.

I once met with a teen who was an absolute genius. The parents, on the other hand, did not have his same level of intelligence and were intimidated by it. In their own insecurity, they rejected and abused him. The pain, confusion, and fear that resulted for this poor teen caused him to become arrogant and obnoxious. Since his parents pushed him away because of his intellect, he felt his intellect was his defining characteristic and held onto it desperately. When he and I talked, I offered him a new idea: that his intellect didn't define him. Even though the trauma he went through felt as personal as could be, it really wasn't personal. It was his parents reacting to their own self-doubts and fears. This teen could now be open to the idea that he could acknowledge his intellect without holding onto it for dear life, that he could be wrong about something or make a mistake and still have just as much value.

Thankfully this message hit home for the teen, and he was able to start healing from his trauma and growing as a person, but he should never have been put in this position. We might not all be as abusive as this teen's parents (at least I sure hope not), but we all do things to inadvertently hurt our children because of our own hurts and issues. We convince ourselves that these are separate parts of our lives and they don't have anything to do with each other, but it's just not true. On a small scale, a parent might have a stressful day at work, so his patience is low when he comes home and he blows up that day about something insignificant. Or on a larger scale, a parent might struggle with his own weight and therefore be overly exacting and critical about every bite the teen puts into his mouth and every pound on his body. These and other situations like them can be devastating for a teenager's life long-term.

Whether it's through therapy, talking to a trusted friend, sometimes medicine, or whatever it is, we owe it to our children to do anything and everything it takes to relieve our own baggage so that we don't end up giving it to them.

Forgetting the "Good" Kids

(First of all, the idea that some kids are good and others are bad is a false concept. We might have feelings one way or another about someone's behavior, but deeming some kids good and others bad is a huge part of why so many of them act out—because by putting such simplistic and often false labels on them, we stop ourselves from really getting to know them, from seeing their behaviors as signs of the deeper things going on.)

We only have so much attention to give at a time, so the kids who don't present problems often don't get much of that attention. They're doing fine, so we focus on the ones who seem to need more help. But what can happen when smart, well behaved, responsible teens go unnoticed?

Dear Mr. Rosenthal,

Throughout the past two years of my life, I had many ups and downs. As every teenager, there are many times I was emotionally unstable, needed someone to hear my problems, or sometimes just needed guidance. You, Mr. Rosenthal, helped me with all.

There are times in life when you think there is nothing left. Everyone is out to get you. Your parents have disowned you. All your friends abandoned you. A guy is completely crushing your self-image. Your family has no money. You have to get over a loss. There is no one who has got it worse.

Having such feelings can have many effects. You can start to seclude yourself, put up a barrier so no one can hurt you. You can become an angry person and become resentful to the people who care for you most. In normal circumstances, one would fall into these traps, but fortunately, our school had the privilege to have a happy teenage life due to the guidance and assurance you gave us.

They say the first step to fixing your problems is acknowledging them. You helped us straight from step one. You helped us make notice of our problems and discomforts. You showed us our shortfalls so that we can be helped from there. When we were ready to be helped, you showed us how we can overcome it, and when we were doing well, you noticed it and encouraged us to go on.

Thank you for everything you gave me and my friends. You helped us through our troubled times and gave us directive to help ourselves in the future. You helped me find my path. You helped me find myself. There are no words to express my appreciation to you.

Sincerely,
SG, age 17

Alice's Story

Take Alice for example. A top student at her high school, Alice at age eighteen was popular, helpful, and involved in many extracurricular activities. She was a pleasure to be around and a strong positive force in her school and home environments. She seemed primed for future success, and she believed she was the best. She didn't have to work hard for her achievements; life was easy and fun. She was happy, satisfied, and well adjusted.

Teens like Alice do not get into trouble. As a result, they are quite often overlooked when it comes to helping them with their personal and social development.

Alice got a degree and was married by the time she was twenty. She's now a stay-at-home mother of five and works part-time for her husband's successful business. The sample below is from when Alice was thirty-four.

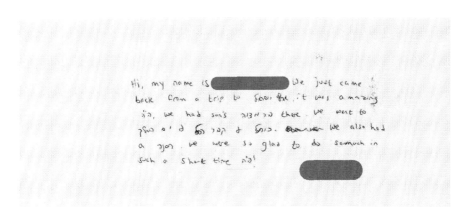

Indicator	Meaning
Clear writing	Good communicator
Messy cross-out	Hides imperfections
Wavy lines across the page	Unclear direction in life
Letters have an uneven pitch (some lean to the left, some to the right)	Insecurity, fear of the future

Large left margin	Feels she's not good enough
Rivers	Defensive
Signature on the far right side of the page	Natural go-getter

In her thirties, life looks and feels different. No longer is Alice in a class of 20 to 50 girls. Her environment now is mainly her home, her husband, and her children. An overwhelmed adult has replaced the carefree teenager she once was. Feeling she's the best (AKA judging others) does not work anymore. Now Alice feels she comes up lacking. She's anxious, nervous, and defensive. She feels she's in the shadow of the shiny pedestal instead of on top of it.

We see all of this in her handwriting. The messy cross-out demonstrates her need to hide her imperfections. The wavy lines across the page show that she is unsure of where she wants to go. The different directions of her writing point to her insecurity and fear of the future. The large left margin is her feeling of not being good enough. The rivers tell us she is defensive. Her signature on the far right of the page shows a natural go-getter. We also see from the clarity in her writing that she's a good communicator, and from her writing speed that she is energetic, generally positive, and highly functional. She likes to be in charge (placement of her signature), but her doubts and insecurities make her feel unworthy. She feels criticized by innocent comments from her husband. She overthinks every decision to the point that every option seems like the wrong one. Instead of enjoying time with friends, being with others only reinforces the idea that she's second best. In her eyes, her old shine is tarnished. She feels hopeless and confused, and she has no idea what to do with her life.

What happened to Alice in these past sixteen years? Her defense mechanism of her youth has now turned into a liability. Judging others when she felt on top worked when she was young and in school. Today, she is still judgmental, but in the reverse: When she was eighteen, she'd believed she was better than her classmates; now she feels she's on the bottom. Because she never learned how to work hard and invest in her success, she's falling apart.

Our attitude about ourselves is in our control. We can choose to respect ourselves and to invest in ourselves, or to let difficult feelings limit our potential. Alice's fixed mindset makes it hard to have a positive, flexible perspective about herself. Feeling that nothing will ever improve, that "I am going to be the same today and tomorrow as I was yesterday," gets depressing. A positive attitude doesn't always just come about as a gift from Heaven; it's a product of effort and hope, which leads to change and flexibility.

This is where my 9 Principles for Living New Possibilities come in. Alice makes two classic mistakes. Firstly, her feeling of not being good enough is a false concept. In truth, there's nothing essentially less-than about Alice; she's only in competition with herself. Secondly, Alice's imperfections do not define her. Rather, they can be seen as opportunities to grow and learn new skills. The act of trying to improve—in and of itself—creates a new skill and a new achievement. New achievements brought about by effort and energy create joy, and joy expands our mindset, increasing hopefulness and flexibility. Nurturing the self-increases self-respect. Flexibility and security make a person happy. The happy person is better able to affect both his immediate environments and the world.

In other words, the simple act of *trying* to change can make Alice's life totally different. Even if her circumstances don't change, just the effort alone can make Alice a new person.

Alice needs to believe that she is great just the way she is. Mistakes don't define her. Someone else's strength doesn't make Alice deficient.

Bottom line: Alice needs to know that she alone is responsible for, and capable of achieving, her own happiness.

It's a certain kind of tragedy that she had to spend half her lifetime feeling small, sad, and powerless. It didn't have to be that way. It's not too late; she can still learn these critical lessons and turn her life around. But it sure would have been nice if she'd learned them when she was eighteen.

Dear Mr. Rosenthal,

I want to thank you for helping me to understand myself better. You helped me deal with some of the problems I was going through this year and get a better understanding of myself. There were a lot of issues I didn't know how to deal with, or so I thought. You showed me that I do know how to help myself, much more than I realized. That could actually be the most important thing you taught me. Because if I can help myself, I can get through anything in life. I wish you lots of success in helping other people my age "find themselves." Our mixed up generation needs people like you!

Sincerely,
SR, age 20

Section II

Living New Possibilities

CHAPTER 5

Living in the Real World (But Not the Way You Think)

NTIL NOW, WE'VE SPOKEN about how teens' brains work, how we adults can take that knowledge and use it to foster loving, trusting relationships with our teens so that they'll be open to our guidance. Now that we've set that secure foundation, you can begin implementing some specific messages that all teens (and adults, too!) can benefit from. My 9 Principles for Living New Possibilities are a set of simple ideas that I found myself coming back to over and over again as I've coached teens throughout the years. Many teens have approached me weeks or years later to tell me that these Principles opened their eyes and changed their lives.

Your Thoughts Create Your Reality
(But You Can Control Your Thoughts)

One common theme runs throughout all 9 Principles: staying in the present moment of truth instead of living within the subjective world of thought. People's thoughts are the thing that holds them back more than anything else—not their circumstances, their history, or even their genetics. Each person's individual life is filled with endless possibilities and powers, but our own fears, worries, and anxiety cause us to get in our own way. We treat our thoughts as if they were physical, irrefutable facts, but our thoughts are only thoughts; they are subject to our perspective and are not pure truth. If we would remove our thoughts from our lives, the facts about our lives would still be the same. We might waste years of our lives worrying about something that never even ends up happening, or we might base all our happiness on the hope of something that never comes to be, or we might spend all our time lamenting the loss of something we can never get back. Life takes its own path that might or might not have anything to do with our thoughts. Living in those thoughts is such a tragic waste of life. Our actions and the present moment are all we truly have.

Thinking is only done in the present. Our brains see time only in the present. Remembering the past and the planning for the future are healthy behaviors that are performed in the present. Emotions people feel about the past or future are also felt in the present moment. We can access memories or make plans without projecting false images onto our story. Even seemingly negative experiences can be experienced in productive ways that are true to the present and don't betray our goals, our desires, and the way we see ourselves and our lives.

A person's thoughts don't have to be to his detriment. You and your teens can use your thoughts to your advantage by actively living in "the real world." This doesn't mean merely growing up; it means staying aware of the facts of the present moment *separate from* our feelings about them. The more we do this, the more we can access the true potency of every moment, unbridled by the false limitations of worry and insecurity.

It bears repeating that most adults don't live in "the real world" the way I'm describing, either. It's not a natural state of being; it's one that must be learned and trained. It's not something that can be expected of someone who hasn't been taught it or had the skill nurtured. So obviously, the earlier someone starts learning how to become present, the better. Teens learning this skill are at an amazing advantage because they will have a major head start in their lives, and adults can be there so much better for their teens with these skills, as well. (In fact, I might venture to say that being present is required in order to fully be there for your teens.) The 9 Principles for Living New Possibilities are tools that all human beings can use to embrace reality without getting too overwhelmed to act, to live!

How many times have you worried and worried and worried about something, then worried some more, to the point where that thing became enormous in your mind and just kept getting bigger, and then when you actually finally dove in and did the thing that scared you, it wasn't even a big deal? How many times did the thing actually get worse *because* of your worrying? We worry about messing up, about what other people will think, about whether we're making the right decision...and in the meantime, our lives are just sitting there, stagnating, growing bacteria and mold, waiting to be lived. Don't let this happen to your teens. Don't let this happen to you.

The Principles are listed below in random order, and one isn't more important than the other. I won't necessarily discuss all 9 Principles with each teen; I usually just pick a couple that seems most relevant to his life, what he needs to hear in that particular moment. These are usually new concepts for them, which sets up a fascinating new paradigm. The healing or improvement occurs in what I call "the long short way";[3] the teen is exposed to a new Principle, which, on an intellectual level, he might grasp quickly, but then it's up to him to do the work, to own the concept. The purpose of the 9 Principles is only to start a conversation, to get the teen to start asking questions, maybe even to feel a little uncomfortable, and to consider the possibility... *maybe there's a different way of looking at life than the way I've been looking at it.*

---

3   Term originally coined in *The Tanya* by Rabbi Schneur Zalman of Liadi.

The 9 Principles for Adults

Before teaching these Principles to your teens, you as the parent or educator will need to embrace them yourself. Easier said than done, since worry tends to affect the things we care about most, and what do we care more about than our children? Parents and educators are rightly occupied with thoughts about their teens' futures. *Will he go to college? Will people respect him? Will he get addicted to cigarettes, or maybe drugs? Will he always be shy? Will he ever learn to dress properly?* The neverending list of unknowns can cause a similarly neverending onslaught of negative emotions.

But these emotions are totally useless and baseless. No one knows what's going to happen in the future. Look at the concept of statistics. Population statistics are used to understand trends and help forecast tendencies. They are the best guesses, but they *cannot* predict what will happen to any individual.

> *A young girl was walking along a beach upon which thousands of starfish had been washed up during a terrible storm. When she came to each starfish, she would pick it up, and throw it back into the ocean. People watched her with amusement.*
>
> *She had been doing this for some time when a man approached her and said, "Little girl, why are you doing this? Look at this beach! You can't save all these starfish. You can't begin to make a difference!"*
>
> *The girl seemed crushed, suddenly deflated. But after a few moments, she bent down, picked up another starfish, and hurled it as far as she could into the ocean. Then she looked up at the man and replied, "Well, I made a difference to that one!"*
>
> -Adapted from "The Star Thrower" by Loren Eiseley

Statistically, it was unlikely for any of those starfish to be saved. Statistics can be useful in planning, but they also cause so much unnecessary stress for individuals. Any one of us could be one of those saved starfish.

Karen's story is an example of how a mother's fear for her teen can backfire. Karen is a 14-year-old sophomore in high school. Her mother worries about Karen's future and gets angry and frustrated with Karen as a result. Karen feels criticized; she does not trust her mother or speak openly with her. Because of the way Karen is viewed by her mother, Karen has learned to hear others' opinions as attacks. The mother, on the other hand, believes Karen is just a difficult 14-year-old.

I love gong to the beach with my family and eating together. I feel very close to my cousin.

The upper horizontal bar in a person's personal pronoun I (PPI) represents the writer's relationship with his or her mother. If you look at Karen's PPI, you'll see that the right side of that top bar is missing, indicating a lack of communication between Karen and her mother. Karen also creates vertical columns called "rivers," indicating that she doesn't feel it's safe to let anyone get close to her. Rivers say, "you stay on your side of the river, and I'll stay on mine."

Karen's behaviors are a nurture problem, not a nature problem. If Karen's mom would learn to lighten up on Karen and stop worrying about things she can't control, Karen would likely feel much safer and able to have a close relationship with her mother, and with other people in general.

Teens feel negativity from the adults in their lives very acutely, which makes them afraid and distrusting. You can and will be far more effective as an adult role model if you can use your thoughts to stay present for what's actually going on instead of getting carried away in The Land of What If. For this reason, when you read my 9 Principles for Living New Possibilities, don't just read them in order to teach the information to your teens; read them and use them in your own life, as well.

Now let's get to the Principles.

Dear Mr. Rosenthal,

I wanted to take the time to profusely thank you for aiding in my maturing. Not only have you taught me things about myself that I can perfect, but you have also highlighted my qualities. Every time I had a session with you, I went home that day and really thought about what you said, and I would and still do try to exercise every bit of advice you have ever given me. I think the advice you felt you had to give me, based on reading my handwriting, is important for every growing and maturing person to hear. These things can literally save a person's self-esteem and self-portrait. I sincerely thank you for teaching me more about myself and helping me overcome constant negative feelings about myself, but most of all I thank you for your devotion for each individual personally.

EK, age 18

The 9 Principles for Living New Possibilities

Chapter 6

———

Your Life Force Makes You Great

Principle 1

WHEN A PERSON PASSES away, his hands, feet, and eyes are all still there, but he's not moving anymore. People call this phenomenon different things depending on their orientation: soul, energy source, spark, the list goes on. That's what moves the hand, makes the eyelids flutter, makes the brain think. For the purposes of this book, we'll call it "life force," but you can call it whatever you want. Removing a body's life force results in that body no longer functioning.

According to Kabbalah, the life force within each one of us is a piece of the greater infinite Life Force that animates all living beings and causes everything to exist.

Our bodies are finite objects, yet the life force that animates our bodies is infinite, and its greatness is infinite, as well. The infinity within us makes each of us great just by our existing.

People who don't feel good enough essentially believe that they don't have greatness within them and that they need to create their own greatness by themselves. Kabbalah says this isn't true, that instead of needing to create greatness, we simply need to reveal the greatness we already have within us.

So how do we reveal that greatness? We reveal it with our actions, by doing acts of goodness and kindness, or by learning and implementing spiritual ideas. Bringing goodness into our lives and sharing goodness with others reveals the goodness that's inside of us.

By the way, a person reveals his greatness as a result of his actions in and of themselves, *irrelevant of the results that come about from those actions*. We can only control what we do; we cannot control what happens after that.

Some people do all the right things but don't feel great because they don't see the results they want. This is a false perception. For example, one kid might put all his might into passing a class, but he still fails. Or a girl who is legitimately the best singer and performer in her grade gets passed over for the leading role in the musical because the other girl's mom is best friends with the play's director. Maybe a teenager has parents who are overly exacting and fail to see his value, despite the fact that the teen goes above and beyond to do the right thing and be the best he can be. Things happen every day that threaten to undermine our perception of our greatness, despite the great things we do. But if we look only at the results of our actions, we're forgetting the actions themselves, which is a big mistake. For example, let's say a person becomes elected to a respected position in his community, but what nobody knows is that he cheated and falsified the vote numbers. Is he still great because he won the election? The results are ultimately not the thing that makes you truly great.

An illustrious family dynasty doesn't make *you* great if you don't follow in their footsteps. A high position in your school board doesn't make you great if you don't use that position for the good. A million Instagram followers don't reveal greatness if you aren't spreading light. A person might have more gifts, talents, and skills than anyone else in the world, and yet he chooses to sit in his pajamas all day every day watching TV. His gifts have little to nothing to do with his greatness.

Our infinite life force also gives us infinite potential. No matter what happens in your life, there are always infinite next steps to choose from and directions to go in. It might seem overwhelming, but it's actually incredibly empowering. It doesn't matter what we were born with or where we are or who we know; all we have to do is...do something!

Some people unwittingly choose to cover up their greatness by being unkind to others or to themselves. On the flip side, after a lifetime of revealing our greatness, the more we shine. There are some holy people in the world whose greatness is just oozing through their pores. That's because they've spent so much time revealing the greatness within them that it's literally visible to those around them.

When people live this way, they glow. When people believe in their own power, they do whatever it takes to be their best selves, and they pay no attention to the things they can't control. These people have an irresistible quality about them that makes people want to be around them, want to know their secret, want to feel the way *they* feel.

The real secret is that anyone can choose to feel this way.

To my knowledge, these students' panels are very accurate. You really captured the essence of their struggles and the underlying core issues.

Dena Gorkin, High School Principal

CHAPTER 7

Healthy Ego

Principle 2

THERE ARE SO MANY misconceptions about the ego. Many people think that having any positive thought about the self is bad. People think that in order to be their best, they need to focus on their flaws and put themselves down. Or they see someone they admire and try to be just like them, and then they hate themselves when they don't succeed.

First of all, being your best has nothing to do with putting yourself down. Actually, that's a great way to make sure you're *not* your best. You need to like yourself, to feel good about who you are, if you want to improve yourself. Seems counterintuitive? Think about your life force. If you know you have a life force that makes you great simply by you existing, how can you put yourself down? To know your greatness is to believe in your greatness, and to feel good about that.

There are always those who ask, *but isn't that egotistical? Aren't I supposed to be humble?* Well, yes, it's good to be humble, but being humble doesn't mean putting yourself down. It means not being full of yourself. It means not using your strengths to gain fame or take advantage of others. It means acknowledging your strengths so that you can put them to good use! It's not egotistical; it's practical. It's real. Some people, in the name of being humble and nullifying their ego, make themselves so small that they practically cease to exist. Now tell me, how can you achieve humility if you don't even exist? You can't be humble if you have nothing to be humble *about*. Know your strengths and do something great with them; now you have a reason to be humble!

Many sweet, kind teens get worked up about the fact that, even though they treat others with respect and dignity, they still *think* negative thoughts about others, or they still think that they're better than others. Isn't that arrogant[4] and egotistical? I tell them to relax. They're OK. Arrogance isn't really arrogance until it's bounced off of someone else. Those thoughts are private. They're not harming anyone. True arrogance doesn't exist until we act on those feelings or speak them into being. Would it be better if we didn't think those thoughts? Sure. But if that's the biggest problem you've got, you're doing great. Don't let this small imperfection get in the way of being your best self.

A healthy ego is crucial to being your best self, to reveal as much of your greatness as possible. Spend some time getting to know yourself. What are your passions, your quirks, the things you love, the things you hate? What are you really good at? What could you improve? What's unusual about you? What quality do you have that nobody else has?

---

4   It is worth noting that arrogant behavior is a sign of not having a healthy ego. Underneath their seeming confidence, these people are actually insecure and feel they have something to prove. So many teens and adults fall for the act of an arrogant person, never realizing how sad the person is inside. If we can instill in our teens the understanding that arrogant people (or, really, people with any seeming personality "defect") are almost always acting out of fear, it would feel like much less of a personal affront when the person is acting in a way that seems offensive. It's really the "arrogant" person's issue. "It's not me, it's you." Really!

Comparing

You were created with your own unique mission and gifts to offer to the world. This is why it's so sad and futile to compare ourselves to others or to try to be like someone else; it's a monumental waste of our true potential. Our job is to offer *our own* gifts, not someone else's gifts! The more unique something is, the more value it has. That's why a painting can cost millions while a poster of that same painting only costs a few bucks. Instead of wasting your energy fighting who you are, embrace your differences and be the best *you* that you can be.

We all have different histories and environments, along with different talents and strengths. Comparing is just not reliable because each person comes with far too many different and complex circumstances. That's why accurate scientific studies are so difficult to do well—so often, there are way too many variables to make certain conclusions. We also tend to see whatever reinforces our perspective, even if it's not true. For example, for people who think they're not as good as others, they tend to minimize their own positive traits and make their own shortcomings huge, while for others they exaggerate their strengths and blow off their flaws. The reality is that everyone, even people who don't seem like it on the outside, has things they struggle with. That's just part of being human. There will always be something you're not as good at, and there will always be something you're better at than someone else. So when you take everyone's entire picture into consideration, you'll see that you're not just not on the same playing field, but you're not even really playing the same game. It's like apples and oranges. There's just no point in comparing.

Even if your comparisons lead you to believe you're "better than," you'll still lose out in the end. All comparisons cause negativity and create defense mechanisms. "Better than" comparisons might seem to work for a while, especially while in school and around classmates, but as soon as you're in your 20's, this falls apart. You basically have two sets of people in your life: people who love you unconditionally (family, close friends), and people who aren't so close to you and don't care much about you (colleagues, acquaintances). So what's the point of feeling better than any of these people? Better than whom? People who don't care about you and you don't care about? Or maybe you feel you're better than your family, your spouse, your children? Why would you even want to feel that way? It's ridiculous. It's messed up. It doesn't work.

Even if you try to be just like someone else, you will fail. Not because you're a loser, but because it's impossible. It is nature's way that no two things can possibly be exactly alike. Everything in the world is different from everything else in the world and serves a unique purpose, otherwise, why would it need to be created in the first place? Even identical twins, created physically exactly the same, have an infinite number of unique personality traits. It goes against nature to be exactly the same as someone else. When things go against nature, they become deformed, sick, even toxic.

The next question I often get is, *isn't it sometimes a good thing to go against your nature?* So here's an analogy. Let's say a man loves the ocean and envies the hours and hours deep-sea fish get to spend underwater. It goes without saying that humans were not meant to live underwater. *But*...what if the man buys scuba gear? Now he can survive underwater for much longer periods. Isn't that going against his nature? No. Going against his nature would be diving unequipped into the deep sea and expecting to live longer than a very short while. Obviously, that won't work. Using scuba gear is *acknowledging* his nature, what he lacks, and what he needs in order to work *with* his nature.

So it's great to emulate some specific traits that we admire in others, but it can't be in a way of comparison, *Oh, he's so much stronger than I am, I'm such a wimp,* but instead, just notice: *He's really strong. Maybe I'll try putting in some extra time at the gym.* Taking out the comparison allows you to stop with the self-hatred, acknowledge the greatness and infinite potential you already have inside you, and access that greatness by doing great acts that help you reach your goals.

The main thing is to invest in ourselves. Each person only has a limited amount of energy and resources. We can choose to invest energy into defense mechanisms, jealousy, and unrealistic ideals, or we can invest our energy into gaining new information, trying new things, improving our weaknesses, or amplifying our strengths. A strength with no invested energy can't grow. And a weakness with added energy might develop into a strength!

When someone's comparing, it's nice to remind him of those specific traits that make him special and unique. The differences within each one of us is what makes life interesting because they give us our own specific journey.

Feedback from Others

Note that, for a teen, especially for a younger teen, feedback from parents and others is a major part of developing a healthy ego and understanding the self. A person really can't do this on his own until about age 18 or even 21, both from a neurological standpoint and an environmental one. Everyone's traits are influenced by the outside world to one extent or another. Parents often naturally offer their thoughts on their children's strengths, weaknesses, talents, and belief systems, and (assuming it's done without judgement) this is a good thing. I think it's important to have conversations about the things you notice about your teens. You might notice your son has an amazing talent for organizing things around the home, but maybe he doesn't even realize that without being told. Or perhaps your daughter is a natural born leader, but it wouldn't occur to her to run for a leadership position in her youth group unless you suggested it. Maybe your teen has never thought about whether there's a G-d. These are all just examples, but they illustrate some ideas that your teens might benefit from beginning to think about, with a little casual help from you.

There are also indirect ways that your teens will get feedback from you about their identities. For example, when you have made clear that you do not tolerate underage drinking but leave your alcohol cabinet open, your daughter learns you think she's trustworthy. When you regularly don't laugh at your son's jokes, he learns he might not be that funny. The little things even *we* aren't necessarily aware that we do can have a major effect on their perceptions of themselves.

It's normal and good for teens to get feedback from their peers, too. As parents, we'd often like it if our teens learned and listened exclusively to us when it comes to developing their beliefs and personality traits, and we all worry about peer pressure. But some amount of peer pressure on a teenager is actually a healthy part of developing a stance on things and learning what's socially acceptable, how different kinds of interactions feel, how to stand up for himself and others, etc. Plus, when a teen grows up to be 30 or 40, he and his peers will be running the world, and without having had ample interactions with his peers when he was young, he'll have a very hard time working with them as an adult. Peer pressure doesn't exist only in the teenage years. The more support and unconditional love a teen gets from the adults in his life, the more he'll be able to think for himself and stand strong when the pressure from friends is laid on thick, including into adulthood.

Your Feelings Are in Your Control

As mentioned above, younger teens really need outside feedback to help develop a healthy ego. The younger someone is, the less capable he is of controlling his self-perception and his feelings. But the older they get, especially by age 18-21, the more capable they are of taking responsibility for their own attitude about things. This is perhaps the most important factor in having a healthy ego. It's nice to get approval from others, and it can even be helpful, but it should not be essential. Feelings of worth come from within, whether we realize it or not. For example, you probably know someone who everyone compliments all the time for some amazing trait, but the person refuses every compliment and constantly puts himself down. You might also know someone who has the most amazing confidence despite lots of negativity from others.

What happens if someone takes you for granted, or if someone overlooks you? You can use your own inner voice to remind yourself that what *they* do has nothing to do with *you*; that *your* value is not dependent on *them*. We cannot control our external environment, but we can control our internal environment, how we feel being us in our lives. It is definitely not easy, but with time it can be learned. Once you do, you will be amazed at how much more power you will feel in your own life. When you realize that you can't control anything but yourself, you no longer need the outside world to make you feel good. Your value is independent of all factors except for: 1. the fact that you have an incredible Life Force that makes you truly powerful, and 2. the things that you do in your life to make an impact on your inner and outer world. When these realities are at the forefront of your mind, it is immeasurably easier to be the master of your own feelings and perception, and to live a happy, empowered life of meaning and truth.

When a person feels depressed, it's his responsibility to spend some time thinking about why he feels down so that he can help himself feel better. If he feels particularly good one day, it pays to think about the reason for that. If he feels anxious about something, it's important to try to get to the bottom of that feeling, but also to fight it in order to live his life to the fullest.

Please note that younger children are *not* as capable of this. For the sake of *their* healthy ego at *their* age, they very much need protection and reinforcement from those around them. For example, the mother of a six-year-old girl was concerned because the daughter had some noticeable dark facial hair that the other girls in her class were making fun of. The mother asked for some opinions from other moms about what to do. Many mothers responded that the girl was far too young to be thinking about hair removal and that the parents should just teach the girl she's beautiful even with her facial hair. That sounds nice, but the reality is that this solution will do nothing because the kids will keep making fun of her, and at that age she won't be strong enough to fight such a negative feeling about herself that will almost definitely result from such insults. Most *adults* have a difficult time internally challenging insults from others; and these parents are expecting a six-year-old to do something they themselves might not be able to do? Keep in mind that these kinds of experiences can shape a child's life forever. This girl needs an adult to understand where she's coming from, what she's dealing with, what she is and isn't able to process as a child of that age. She needs someone to protect her from things she herself cannot do anything about. In other words, she needs her mom to offer to buy her a bottle of Nair and get that hair removed.

At any age, it's a fine balance between influencing your child and empowering him to take responsibility for his own feelings and experience.

You helped me respect myself and understand that ego isn't a bad thing. It just needs to be utilized in a good way. Putting myself down won't kill the ego. It will just put me in a bad mood in my surroundings. Thank you so much for helping me understand this. You gave me the will and the confidence to be me.

DD, age 18

CHAPTER 8

Be the Best You Can Be
In the Moment

Principle 3

ALL WE HAVE IS THE PRESENT. We can't change the past, and we can't predict the future. We can think about the past and the future, and we can use them to learn from to experience joyful or painful emotions, but we can't change them. Since the brain doesn't know time and we function in the present, when we think about the past or the future, we're always doing it in the present moment. The only thing we can do anything about, even in terms of just our thoughts, is this moment, right now.

This concept is particularly interesting to me. It's so basic, but most people initially just don't get it. The usual knee jerk reaction to the idea of being the best you can be in this moment is, *I could be better.* That's true. We all could be better. But until this moment, you were the best you could be. Actually, from the perspective of the present, everything that happened until now was both the best *and* worst it could be. It just is. You can't change anything that happened up until now. Your circumstances are the best they could be because they're *all* that could be, because you cannot change the past. Walking down the street and you fall in the mud: best you could be in that moment. Do you like being in the mud? No. Do you like the result of being in the mud? No. But that's what happened. You are now in the mud. So be it. Now's your opportunity for making things better. You can invest your energy into picking yourself up. Now you have choices for making things the best they can be, given your current circumstances. Should you go back home and change, or do you continue on your way? Whatever you decide to do, once it's done, that's the best you could have been in that moment. You decide you need to go on your way in muddy clothes because you're in a rush: best you could have been in *that* moment. Or, you'll be a little late and go back home and change: best you could have been in *that* moment.

Since you cannot control the past or future, dwelling on them is futile. The past and future are only tools to be used in the present. It's good to acknowledge what you could have chosen to do better so that next time maybe you'll choose differently if necessary. But feeling upset or less-than due to past choices, feeling like you're not the best you could be, makes no sense. Every single moment provides you with the power to make the best choice *currently* available to you. *That* is being the best you can be in the moment. Life is a series of making choice after choice based on circumstance and prediction. Acknowledge your current circumstances (past), use statistics to plan out your options as best you can (future), and then do what seems like the best choice (present). What happens after that is out of your control.

Part of why people have a hard time accepting this concept is because they amplify the negative events of their past to the extent that they become paralyzed in the present. Consider the fact that the way we remember past events is rarely if ever totally accurate. When a person recalls major negative emotional events from the past, those emotions are changed to fit the person's present age, maturity, and understanding of the world and his life. An eight-year-old's disappointment doesn't match an eighteen-year-old's disappointment. But when an eight-year-old experiences a major disappointment, and then ten years later he remembers that event, the now eighteen-year-old upgrades that memory and experiences the disappointment as he would have had it happened when he was eighteen. The way he's experiencing that memory is not real. It might appear real, but it's not the same disappointment of that eight-year-old boy. The emotion is no longer purely the eight-year-old's emotion and fixed in time. The further we are from the event, the less accurate and precise our memory of it is likely to be. There will be a certain amount of distortion for an event that happened even as recently as yesterday or five minutes ago; how much moreso for an event that happened many years ago.

I don't belittle people who are suffering with past emotions. I'm just describing the phenomenon. I'm not naive enough to think that neutralizing major emotional events is easy or simple. But what I'm describing isn't my opinion; it's a generally accepted standard of psychology.

We also often build up positive memories of the past way more than was actually true. For example, a girl might long for an ex-boyfriend who she remembers as the most incredible guy in the world, when the reality that she forgot, but was very aware of while it was happening, was that he was neglectful, uninteresting, and often rude.

Knowing this, we can make the present moment better by not getting overly caught up in the emotions attached to our memories. For one, the memories themselves are almost certainly not entirely accurate, and in any case, being halted by the emotions attached to our memories is never a good thing.

Being the best you can be in the moment is also the same with regard to what's going to happen in the future. You can only do the best you can do right now, and no matter what you choose, you cannot control what will happen after that. Planning is a good thing, but *worrying* about what will happen in the future is a false concept. You don't know what's going to happen. Use your predictions about the future to be the best you can be in the moment, but don't think of those predictions as facts, and certainly don't amplify them. Weatherman predicts a hurricane? Fine. Plan for your safety. But worrying about that hurricane that's three days away out over the ocean isn't going to help your situation. To the contrary, it will actually halt your ability to do what you need to do. Your brain, not knowing time, thinks the future event that you're worrying about is happening now, and so your brain is wasting its energy now by experiencing unnecessary fear to fight a currently nonexistent situation. Plan for the future and work your plan, but experience your life in the present. Be the best you can be in this moment, no matter what happens after this moment. Don't let your best be lessened out of fear. And if you're just not able to control your fear yet? That's also part of your circumstances. Own it, and move forward. With your fear, be the best you can be.

Hi Yaakov,

I just wanted to thank you for your wonderful presentation to the AHAF Study Group tonight! What a great way of approaching the teenagers. Your sensitivity to their age of development is a great reminder to all of us.

Valerie Weil, Certified Graphologist

CHAPTER 9

Don't Let Your Strength
Be a Weakness

Principle 4

S O OFTEN, WE BELIEVE that our greatness is demonstrated through our strengths in and of themselves. We've already discussed that a strength has no inherent greatness unless it's used for the good. In this section, we'll discuss the problem that can arise when the *opposite* of a person's strength needs to be performed, or when that person needs to refrain from performing his strength. For example: some people give excellent advice, but there are times when even the wisest person needs to keep his advice to himself. When this person defines himself solely by his strengths, then he doesn't believe he's great anymore when he's not giving advice. *If I'm not sharing my wisdom, what am I?*

Sometimes you need to do something you're not good at, or something that isn't usually in your best interest. But for some people, the resistance to doing so can feel so strong that it seems like a matter of survival. I am reminded of a young woman whose father was very sharp, rude, and flat out just saying not nice things to her for no reason. When the girl approached him about it, the father's response was, "Well, I say things like they are. It's served me very well all my life, and I'm not going to stop now." When she suggested to him that perhaps different qualities are appropriate for different occasions, that perhaps sometimes it's better to be gentle and to *not* say what's on his mind, he couldn't accept that. The girl later found out that her father had been molested repeatedly as a child by someone close to him. I'm sure he learned then and there that being gentle and quiet were not good qualities if he wanted to stay safe.[5]

Maturity is knowing when to apply which characteristic and then doing it. He'd be better off if he could accept that being blunt is *sometimes* a good quality instead of *always*. It's a defense mechanism that he literally didn't know how to survive without.

If this girl's father hadn't defined himself by his ability to "say things like they are," maybe he'd have a closer relationship with his daughter and other people in his life. His traumatic life experiences taught him that it wasn't safe to be gentle, and that tact was not only useless but also dangerous. He perceived directness as a strength, and the opposite as a weakness. It would benefit him to learn that his perceived strength is actually a weakness at times, and also that his perceived weakness could sometimes be used as a strength.

It can be scary to do something you're not used to doing, but that doesn't mean you shouldn't do it. When the circumstances call for performing a weakness or for not performing a strength, it doesn't take away from who you are. In fact, it makes you greater. Not defining ourselves by any particular trait allows us to have far fewer limitations in life, and to be more capable and make the best choice in any given moment.

---

5 This young woman's ill treatment by her father started only once she was already a young adult; she had a healthy childhood and a good relationship with her father until the couple of years preceding this story. Perhaps it was because she didn't have a lifetime of trauma built up that she was able to have such clarity of mind to speak to her father the way she did. Otherwise, she probably wouldn't have had the strength for that.

Instead of feeling insecure about doing things that aren't strengths of yours, just see them as opportunities to grow or to do things you don't usually get to do. Investing time and energy into defense mechanisms takes away that time and energy from learning the actual lesson and overcoming challenges. Also, the fewer defenses a person has up, the wider his personality can be, and the more variety he has in way to express himself. The more environments in which he can express himself, the more of that person's greatness is revealed.

Your Weaknesses Can Be Strengths

It's a positive thing to understand what our strengths and weaknesses are. It's defining ourselves by them that's the problem. We are constantly changing. Each moment requires something different from us. Sometimes we need to do something we're not good at. And just because you're not good at something now doesn't mean you won't ever be. If you aren't a good runner, you can train and become one. If you lack social skills, you can develop them. To consider a weakness that you have as a static, unchangeable thing is to limit yourself immensely. Most people can improve at most things if they have a positive attitude and put in enough effort. It might not even be that hard.

By the way, *weakness doesn't mean bad*. Think of a chart where not being skilled at something is the baseline, and then some people are more talented/skilled at that thing, so they rise above the baseline. But there's nobody *beneath* the baseline, meaning, baseline is normal. *Most people are weak at most things*. Which means that weakness is the baseline, and normal. Most people are skilled/talented at only a *small* number of things, so they rise above the baseline there. But if you have a chart listing every possible skill, most people will fall at the baseline for most skills and above for only one or a few skills.

You helped me realize and become conscious of who I am and what I need to work on. Your advice was very practical, and I am using it every day. You didn't overwhelm with words and ideas. You went straight to what I need to know and how I should work on it, and I really appreciate that.

Thank you,
SK, age 19

CHAPTER 10

Happy Rule

Principle 5

I MAGINE YOU'RE IN A ROOM with 10 paintings. Two of them are just exquisite, three of them are really nice, two of them are fine, two of them aren't your taste, and one you find just awful. Now imagine you had to stay in that room for the rest of your life. Would you spend all your time, or most of your time, or even much of your time at all on the one painting that you hate? You might check it out from time to time, but you'd probably spend most of your time on the paintings you love the most. So why do we do the opposite when it comes to the real events in our lives?

If you would make a list of all the things that occur in your life every day, from the littlest things to the biggest things, the vast majority of things on your list would probably range from neutral to pleasant. Then there are moments that are rotten, people who bother you, instances that aren't fun, surprises that don't go well, causing tension or stress. There's a general principle that negativity pierces and positivity surrounds. Negative events tend to have a stronger impact on us than positive ones.

Take the example of going to a fancy restaurant. You order an appetizer, a soup, a main course, and a delicious dessert. Everything is scrumptious. Everything. Even down to the spicy mayo. However, the vegetables were overcooked, just not tasty. You don't eat them. The steak, the fries, the salad, the soup, the appetizers, and the luscious double chocolate ice cream dessert—unbelievable. You get up to leave, and you see a friend coming in. He asks you, how was the restaurant? Most people will say, "It was really good, but watch out for the vegetables; they burned them." Now, the vegetables were irrelevant to the whole meal. You didn't go to the restaurant for them. If they hadn't given them to you, you wouldn't have missed them. Had they switched them up, you wouldn't have known. But these vegetables, because negativity is piercing, took on the same weight as the steak, the fries, the salad, the soup, and the dessert combined.

Our job is to make the negative only as noisy as it deserves to be. If our life is made up of 80 percent positive experiences and 20 percent negative ones, instead of harping on the 20 negative, remember that you have 80 positive! You can choose to listen to the noise of the 80 percent good instead of the 20 percent bad. Live with the perspective of the joy that makes up the majority of your life. The goal is to bring the positive inside of you and to keep the negative on the outside.

When negative things do occur, find ways to draw positivity out from them. Invest some energy and see if you can improve them, by actually changing the situation, by learning what to do differently in the future, or even just by understanding or accepting that there are times when life does not go the way you'd like it to go.

The point is that our thoughts, our focus, create our reality. If we focus on the 20 percent negative, our reality will be negative, and if we focus on the 80 percent positive (which logically, mathematically, makes sense anyway because 80 percent is the majority), our reality will be positive and pleasant and happy. So even though our life is not largely negative, if we *focus* largely on the negative, it will be negative.

Parents and teachers, this is not an excuse to judge your teens' feelings or perception of their world. When they're feeling like everything is dark, telling them to focus on the positive will probably do nothing but make them feel misunderstood and more upset. Rather, this is a lesson to teach through example, or to mention casually while *not* in times of darkness or upset. In the moment, just validate your teen's experience without trying to teach.

Excellent description of my student over the years I've known him. I understand now how you were advising me with him.

Moishe Lieblich, High School Principal

Chapter 11

Mistakes Don't Define You

Principle 6

EACH HUMAN BEING IS infinitely complex. A person's identity has countless facets and can't be defined by any one characteristic, event, or action. This is why it should be (but definitely isn't) obvious that a person is not defined by his mistakes, just like he's not defined by anything else. The problem is that teens are much more aware than they ever were of the fact that people judge each other, and that their actions have consequences. It doesn't help that most of their peers and friends wouldn't dare share that they also have struggles and mess things up sometimes, and the fake airbrushed social media world in which teens are so deeply entrenched only makes things worse. As a result, each teeanger thinks he's the only one in the world going through hard times and making mistakes, and then when a teenager does make a mistake, he feels like *he is the mistake*. So he worries, sometimes to the point of drama or true panic, about what will happen if he makes a mistake. As if the worrying will help. (It won't.) And aside from serving no purpose, worrying also comes from faulty reasoning.

Mistakes are not events that carve a person's identity in stone. They are snapshots of fleeting moments in time. So you made a mistake in this one moment? Okay, but in the moments before that and after that you had successes. So why define yourself by that one mistake? It makes no sense.

Let's say a student gets a 40 on a math test. Does that mean the student is a failure? No! It means that at the specific time during which he took his test, he answered 40 percent of the questions right. That's it. It's not an indication of his intelligence, and it's not even necessarily an indication of his work ethic. There are so many reasons someone might have gotten that grade. He could be a genius history buff, but math isn't his forte. Or maybe he is great in math but was absent for a couple classes and didn't realize he didn't learn some of the material. Maybe he was in class but didn't pay attention because he was upset or excited about something else. Perhaps he paid attention but mistakenly studied the wrong material. Or he paid attention, and he studied the right material, but he studied alone and really needed some guidance. Could be he studied with a friend, but they chatted the whole time and didn't really get anything done. Maybe he did everything right but misunderstood the question. Or maybe he started getting anxious and froze.

Whatever the reason, the 40 doesn't define the student; it just shows how much information he was able to access at that moment. Instead of deeming yourself an idiot or a loser, use the mistake (in this case the 40) to improve yourself. The purpose of the grade is to teach the student what he can work on in order to fix the problem. If you daydream, ask for help to improve your focus. If you studied alone, learn with a friend next time. If you learned with someone but didn't find it helpful, find someone new to learn with. If you misunderstood the questions, spend an extra minute rereading them before answering. Mistakes are learning opportunities. Try to understand why the mistake happened, and invest in improving.

Note that sometimes the thing that needs to be improved upon isn't the mistake itself but just the act of letting go and moving on. If you are at the park one day and a dog runs straight toward you out of nowhere and trips you and you face plant into the gravel, the lesson isn't really "be less clumsy" or "don't trust dogs." It's to get up, brush yourself off, and move on with your life.

What Will People Think?

One of the less pleasant parts of adolescence is realizing two related things: 1. There's a world outside of me, and 2. I'm a part of that outside world. And just like I have opinions about the people in that outside world, other people have opinions about me, too. That brings up a really uncomfortable question... *What are they thinking of me?*

When someone makes a mistake, gets a poor grade on a test, doesn't know the answer, falls down in the mud...when things don't go as planned, the person often has to engage in something that's a weakness instead of a strength. This increases the likelihood of performing poorly. So now, in addition to the normal worries of failure that come with having to do something that is not easy or familiar, there are more worries of the outside world and the thoughts of the people in it.

Now I'm going to let you in on a little secret...the reality is...most of them don't care!

Think of your life like a movie. You are the protagonist, a handful of loved ones are the supporting actors and actresses, one or a few people who don't like you are the antagonists, and the vast majority of other people you see or interact with peripherally are a whole bunch of extras.

The extras, who make up most of the people in your world, are there, but they really don't have anything to do with you, for no real reason except that you're both too busy to get to know each other. Nothing wrong with that.

When a person makes a mistake, those extras, who are a nonessential part of your background, don't care or even necessarily know that there was a mistake at all. If they do know about the mistake, they might even show compassion or empathy. To use the mud example again, if a person falls down in the mud, an extra might think, *Oh my gosh! Is he all right? Yup. Okay, so I'll go back on with my life.* Then there are some extras who might think, *Wow, what a klutz.* Now, does it affect you in any way that when a random person who you don't know and don't care about has a negative thought about you? Rarely. What an extra thinks of you is usually almost entirely irrelevant.

Then there are the antagonists. Whether you make a mistake, get a Nobel Prize, or do something in between, they'll dislike you no matter what. The reality is that there will always be a percentage of people who don't like you, and if you make a mistake, they still won't like you. Their opinion of you doesn't change based on what you do. So it really doesn't pay to worry about what they'll think of your mistakes, because nothing you do will change what they think, anyway.

Same with people who like you. Your friends and family will generally still like you after you make a mistake. And that's easily proven, because when *your* friends make mistakes, you give them a pass. You feel empathy for them. You might even try to help them.

The point is, if you're worrying what people think about your mistakes, stop. Your friends still like you, and the people who don't like you still don't like you, and the people who don't know you don't know anything happened in the first place, and if they do they don't care.

But sometimes someone's opinion of our mistake does *affect us.* True. For example, if your boss thinks you messed up, you might get fired. If the class bully sees you fall in the mud, he might turn the whole class against you so that you have no friends. If you try out for a play and you mess up at the audition, you might not get the part. But in the whole scope of your life, those kinds of situations are not the norm. We're talking about *most* mistakes. The vast majority of mistakes don't matter. Even at most work situations, mistakes are expected, understood, and moved on from.

Other People's Mistakes Also Don't Define You

If a crazy person on the sidewalk mumbled to you that you were a stupid idiot and nobody loved you, would you take it personally? Obviously not, because that person is crazy. The thing is, we're all a little bit crazy sometimes. We all have brain malfunctions, sometimes more often or more extreme than others. Just because someone says something hurtful, that doesn't mean it actually has anything to do with you. If a friend is rude, that friend has issues that need to be worked on. Even people who love you deeply can make extremely hurtful mistakes at your expense. They might think they're doing the right thing, or they might be totally oblivious, or they might be experiencing difficult emotions and acting out of their own pain. Either way, it's not you, it's them.

Even if someone is harshly criticizing you with real things that you really do need to work on, that person's *harshness* is not a reflection of you. The person could have chosen to speak gently and kindly to you and still help you work through the issues you need to address. While the issues themselves might be a reflection of you, the way the person chose to express those issues and the pain the person caused you are a reflection of the other person. It doesn't mean you're awful. It means that person needs to work on himself.

Mr. Rosenthal is the greatest handwriting analyst. He changes lives. Over a period of five sessions this year, I changed completely. Mr. Rosenthal was able to explain my actions and my life through my handwriting. He then showed me right from wrong and helped me choose better. He helped make me into a better person. Thanks!

DV, age 17

CHAPTER 12

The 90-10 Friendship Rule

Principle 7

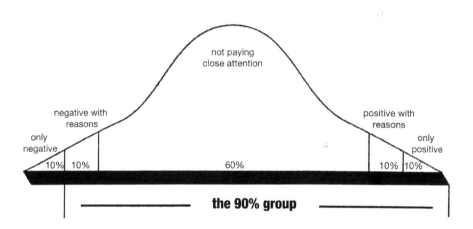

THE 90-10 FRIENDSHIP RULE works like this. If you look at the right side of the bell curve above, you'll see ten percent of people who just love you unconditionally no matter what you do, and another ten percent of people who love or like you conditionally, for specific reasons. Mirrored to that on the left side of the graph are ten percent of people who, for no reason at all, don't like you, and next to that are people who dislike you for some specific reason. The 60 percent in the middle are people who are extras in your movie. They don't like or dislike you; they don't really have much to do with you. You're an extra

in *their* movie, too. Just the way it is. There are only so many hours in a day to get to know people.

In general, this ratio works. Let's say there are 50 people in a teenager's ninth grade class. Of those 50 people, you'll be very friendly with up to five of them, and another five you'll be pretty friendly with; they'll be in your circle, but they won't be your very best friends. So in 50 people, there might be between two and ten people who really like or love you. Most people will have two very close friends, maybe three, and if you're very talkative and like to connect then perhaps five, but no more than that will be really close. On the flip side, there'll be two to ten people who do not like you, some for no real reason, some because of jealousy, some because of a real reason that you could try to change. So that's 20 people whose thoughts are actively involved with you, half positive and half negative. The other 30 people are acquaintances. They know you, they say hi to you, they know where your desk is in the class, but that's about it.

The 90-10 Friendship Rule has two main points. First, if you have two close friends, that's normal. Nothing to be uptight about. If you have one good friend, that's also nothing to be uptight about. Be grateful for that one good friend. Or you might have four or five good friends and one best friend. Relax. It's normal. It's the way it is.

Second: The people who don't like you—also normal. You can't please everybody. Just a normal function of life. When it comes to the ten percent of people who do not like you for no reason, since there's no logic behind why they don't like you, you'll never make them like you no matter what you do. It just is. The other ten percent who don't like you have reasons for it. These people might be messengers in disguise. You might not like what they have to say, but it might be of importance. Maybe there's a good lesson for you to learn. These people become like mailmen. They might be delivering junk mail, or the mail might be of value. That's for you to determine.

Most of us, and especially teens, tend to focus on worrying about the ten percent of people who we will never be able to please. How senseless, when it's an almost negligible percentage to begin with, and we can't do anything about them, anyway! Stop wasting your time and energy, remove that ten percent from your thoughts, and get your feedback from people who have something relevant to say. The majority of people in your life love you no matter what, or really like you, or don't have anything to do with you, or might have helpful constructive criticism to offer. In other words, there's no point in worrying about the people in your world. Just relax, be yourself, and do the best you can in your life.

To Mr. Rosenthal,

I want to take this time out to offer my deepest thanks for helping me the way you have. Before I met you, I was going through life with a shallow understanding of the reasons behind my feelings and behaviors. You have clarified a lot of things for me, things that, for a young girl, are too complicated to understand on my own.

I also want to thank you for dedicating your time to helping me better myself. The fact that you take time out of your day to enhance mine is so praiseworthy. Because of your work, I have become very interested in handwriting analysis, and am currently reading a book on it.

Thank you for caring and giving me tools to help myself. I believe that the biggest thing a person can do for another is to help them help themselves. (Instead of giving a man a fish, teach him how to fish.)

I appreciate your efforts.

Sincerely,
MG, age 14

CHAPTER 13

False Concepts

Principle 8

W<small>E ARE ALL BIASED</small> to one degree or another to expect certain things from our surroundings based on our experiences, what other people do, what we see in movies, what we read in the news and in books, etc. While it's normal to have these expectations as a result of what we've been exposed to, they cannot be counted on as facts or ultimate truths. The problem is when we treat them as if they were. Then, when things don't go as we'd expected, we experience unnecessary disappointment, frustration, anger, stress, and hopelessness.

For example, your teen might think that if he fails math, he won't get into a good college, which means he'll always struggle as an adult. This is a false concept. Sure, many people who do poorly in math might have a hard time getting into college, but there's no hard and fast rule that it will absolutely be that way, and anyway, college isn't the end-all-be-all of success. Plus, plenty of people are brilliant in one area and null in another, and they make their success in their areas of strength.

You might believe that your teenager will (Heaven forbid) get lung cancer if he takes up smoking. True, statistically, cigarettes are not good for you. But we're not statistics. We're individual people. Some people live to 90 years old smoking a pack a day. So, where you're correct that cigarettes often cause people harm, it's a false concept that it *will* cause your son harm.

It's normal to feel concerned about potential negative consequences of something that often turns out bad. But getting caught up in those worries is the problem. The ensuing stress inhibits us from being present and from reacting to issues in ways that could actually be helpful. Plus, ultimately, we do not know what's going to happen in the future, nor can we control it. We can only make the best choices we can with the information and tools we have, but what happens after that is out of our hands.

You Shouldn't Should

Living without false concepts is living in the moment, living in reality. "Shoulds" and "should nots" must be majorly limited.

For example, you might believe that children *should* respect their parents. This is another false concept. It is nice for parents when children respect them, but that's it. The reality is that children won't always respect their parents, and there's no real way to enforce it with certainty.

A teenager might feel that his mother shouldn't scream at him when he's two minutes past curfew. Well, of course he'd rather she not do that, and perhaps none of his friends' mothers would do that, and perhaps it *is* an overreaction. But none of that changes the fact that his mother is who she is, and his opinion about it doesn't change her.

When we get caught up in false concepts, and then something goes against one of these false concepts, the result is unnecessary anger and often trying to change things to fit our belief system. Unfortunately for us, not everything *can* be changed to fit our belief system. The only thing we actually have control over is ourselves. So, in trying to control something we have no control over, we waste our time and energy while we could be making actual change somewhere where it'd be helpful.

Take for example, a girl I met who had a very rocky relationship with her mother. The girl felt her mom was selfish, immature, and generally unaware of the world around her. The daughter moved out as soon as she was old enough and, hoping for some respite, set a lot of boundaries with her mom...and I mean *a lot*. The daughter told her mother when and how many times a day she could call and text, how often they could see each other, what topics of conversation she'd allow, etc. The mother never really got the clue and continued to call whenever she wanted and as often as she wanted about whatever she wanted. This infuriated the daughter to the point that she would respond with harsh, angry text messages and even threatened to cut off all communication. Because the mom continually and predictably went against her daughter's wishes, the daughter felt indignant and disrespected. She felt her mother *should* act a certain way: false concept. She tried to enforce her rules, and time and time again, it didn't work, which just made her angrier. Because...that's what happens with false concepts.

What might have happened if the girl let go of her false concept about what mothers *should* be, and she accepted her for who she is (albeit with some disappointment)? What if, instead of telling her mom to stop calling so frequently, she told her mom nothing but only answered the phone when she felt it was a good time? What if, instead of telling her mother what she was and wasn't allowed to talk about, she simply changed the subject when a topic came up that she wasn't comfortable with? What if, instead of threatening to cut off communication if her mother didn't adhere to her rules (which likely put her mother into a panic and made her act out in desperation, aside from the fact that her mother was clearly not capable of adhering to those rules in the first place), she set up rules for *herself* to follow that would keep her feeling healthy, sane, and capable of having a somewhat peaceful relationship with her mother? Maybe if she stopped expecting her mother to be or do anything, she would also stop feeling so disappointed and angry when her mother didn't live up to her expectations.

This sad story exemplifies just how counterproductive false concepts are. They keep us from actually dealing appropriately with what *is*. How many years did this girl waste trying to force her mother into actions that were never going to happen? On feeling hopeless? On feeling angry?

Getting angry about something gives us a false sense of power over that thing. But the truth is that our emotions and thoughts don't give us power over anything. Only our actions give us power…. And some things *still* will not be changed by our power, no matter what we do.

That's not to say that a person isn't entitled to disappointment or upset when they don't like something in their lives. But trying to change something you can't change is pointless. Allow yourself to feel disappointed, assess whether there's something you *can* change (within yourself, never expecting something of someone else), and move forward.

G-d,
Grant me the serenity to accept the things
I cannot change,
The courage to change the things I can,
And the wisdom to know the difference.

-Reinhold Niebuhr

Over 2 years ago I had a small 10 minute handwriting analysis and discussion with Mr. Rosenthal and it was a life changing experience!! Now after speaking to Mr. Rosenthal a few times I can say that I've definitely gained a lot of direction and confidence from his incredible talent and knowledge. I feel that Mr. Rosenthal is a incredibly grounded person, that he really feels what what people need in order to improve and grow.

MM, age 18

CHAPTER 14

Be Present for the Process

Principle 9

I OFTEN ASK PEOPLE THE QUESTION, "If there are 2,000 steps in a mile, which step is the most important?" Many people answer either the first step or the last, the first being the momentum to begin, and the last being the destination. Actually, they're all important. Without step 63, you can't get to 64, and you might slip around step 700 and take a little time to recover. But you still need that step to get to 701 and 702.

This whole journey, from beginning to end and everything in between, is where the learning, flexibility, confidence, and happiness reside. Feel good about your process. Feel good about taking step 1 and step 2 and step 1,377. Work hard. Finally, you'll reach the destination.

And...every destination is followed by the *next* destination, the next mile and the next mile. It feels good to reach a destination, but if that's the only source of joy, being that we usually are *striving* for the destination but only spend a small amount of time actually *at* any destination itself, most of the time you'll feel unsatisfied. Not to mention that living solely for destinations often causes us to build up our expectations far past what's actually reasonable, only to crash big time when the reality doesn't match up with what we'd imagined.

The reason so many people live for the destinations is because those are the "big deal" moments, as opposed to the seeming minutiae in between. It's natural and fine to anticipate your goals. This helps us plan and gives us reason to *make* goals in the first place. At the same time, the journey itself is also filled with excitement, pleasures, learning opportunities, connections with others, growth, etc. If we only focus on the destination, we'll miss all the incredible moments that happen before we even get there. I would venture to say, for example, that most people get way more out of the compilation of moments in 4 years in college than they do out of their graduation day. Yes, graduation is nice, and it's the goal. But in the meantime, so many lifelong friendships are made, so many skills and lessons are learned, so many good times are had. If you don't make yourself present for those moments, and allow them to happen in the first place, it's easy to get caught up in tunnel vision and miss out on life's biggest opportunities for growth, learning, and joy.

Every day, live in the moment. Be present while you take your steps, make mistakes, and grow. Feel good that you're on your unique trip one step at a time, sometimes with others, sometimes by yourself, sometimes using plan B or plan C, but always in the moment. Plan for the future, but live in the moment. The process is just as important as the destination.

Four months ago, I went on a trip to New York. I had heard about Mr. Rosenthal's work. I thought it was very possible that his whole thing was totally fake, but I wanted to see for myself. Little did I know it would completely change my life.

I have always done well in school but never thought very highly of myself. I have somewhat struggled socially and at home with my mom, and I just felt like I was never good enough.

After he looked at my writing for a minute or two, he told me, "You're an 'OWE,' Own Worst Enemy." He told me that despite being very talented, smart, and friendly, I always felt like people didn't like me. He said that I looked at myself with a negative eye, that I didn't do well under pressure, and that I was very hard on myself. He told me, "You need to work on being BFF with yourself." He said my insecurities were making me uptight and hard to be around, and that if I'd just relax and enjoy being the great man I am, people would like to be around me much more.

I was blown away. Everything he said was so pinpoint and accurate, it really spoke to me. So many "good" mentors in school always told me I have to do more and more, but they did not at all see what I personally needed to grow. Mr. Rosenthal spoke with me about what exactly to work on. So I started working on that a lot, and I still work on it now.

Four months later, I see a huge difference in myself, and I know it was triggered by my conversation with him. I see from the way people interact with me now that things are changing. My relationships are much better. I get much more respect from people. I don't feel nervous to approach people I don't know. I don't feel it's out of place for me to talk to someone of importance. The more I work on it, the better I'm getting.

Last year, I was worried for months about my summer plans. Would I get accepted to any of the programs that I applied to? Was I good enough? Now, I have multiple options of programs that are pursuing me to come to them! Just the other day, I bumped into a director for one of the programs I'm considering. Before, I would have been so nervous. This time, he came over to me, to ask me to come to his program!

Mr. Rosenthal is very grounded in the reality of what people are and not what they should be. He taught me that I can acknowledge something for what it is, and still have my opinion, without getting angry about it. This has really helped me a lot in interacting with my mother. I have to be so careful with every word I say to her because she will always twist it around and interpret it in a way that I'm doing something wrong, against her beliefs. I used to get very worked up about her, and lash out, wishing she was different. Now, when she goes on and on about something, I just listen, but still tune in to my feelings. I don't even have to say much, but now she feels respected and heard, and I don't have to get angry or insecure.

Mr. Rosenthal and I have now met three times. I have learned so much about reasonable expectations for myself and how to be there for myself. And I can see that I have changed a lot as a result. His approach transformed me from angry, insecure, and uptight, to more peaceful, relaxed, confident, and happy.

Mr. Rosenthal is not a psychologist, and that's a good thing. What he does is so much better. He really helps people change, fast. I think he is absolutely incredible.

MM, age 18

CHAPTER 15

───────

Trauma and Survival:
A Physical Reality

You've probably encountered teens who are extremely reactive, who act irrationally without thinking, who are so defensive you can't get a word in. It's a natural reaction to be annoyed and feel like this kid just needs to get his act together. But it pays to ask why he's acting this way. Is he naturally annoying and irritating? Is this just normal teenage behavior? Or is something deeper going on?

First of all, **nobody is just naturally obnoxious**. As we've discussed in several places in this book, **people act in ways that are difficult to tolerate when they're reacting to something that's difficult for them.** Second of all, a lot of these kids have experienced trauma that they don't know how to process. It puts them in a state of constant fear, which makes them act out in ways others don't understand.

My 9 Principles for Living New Possibilities can make a world of difference for teens, but if the teen has been traumatized, he usually needs something deeper first.

The point of this chapter is not to explain the entirety of trauma and/or trauma therapy; that's outside of the scope of this book. However, I do want to mention trauma for two reasons. The first is that it gives some insight into the possible reasons some teenagers act and react the way they do. The second is to suggest what I believe to be the best form of treatment.

What Is Trauma?

Trauma occurs when something so deeply disturbs or frightens a person that it makes the person feel unsafe at his core and thereby unable to cope in healthy ways.

What causes trauma? It's different for everyone; for one person it might be his parents' divorce, for another it could be a bad breakup, or being bullied, or being repeatedly yelled at at home, or being falsely accused of cheating by a teacher, or falling off a bike, or being stolen from. It could be literally anything. As said before, something might roll off one person's back but be traumatic for another. It's really up to the person's perception and resilience. For example, in a family with two children where the parents are getting a divorce, one child might be totally fine, while the other might not be able to handle it. There's no way of telling who will react how to different events. For some, time heals, but for others, seemingly nothing heals. What might be traumatic for one person might be so irrelevant for another that he doesn't even register that it happened.

- Whatever it is, when it happens, it can affect people in ways that dramatically affect their day-to-day living and change who they are.

"Trauma has the power to occupy so much of our body, nervous system, and energy that we have little or no room for pleasure," says Dr. Regalena Melrose in her book *Why Students Underachieve.* "We cannot contain joy with comfort and ease. We are left with such humiliation, shame, and fear that we do not believe that pleasure can be ours, that it can last, or that we deserve it. Hence, our traumatized students turn away from compliments, find a quick way to discount praise, or sabotage a moment that seemed to bring them some peace or pride. It is important to recall that this is not a cognitive process. This is about the body's capacity to contain and tolerate excitation that rises in the nervous system when noticed and complemented by others."

Trying to Survive

Whatever the source, trauma goes deeper than cognitive thought. Because the traumatized person is feeling threatened, his basic survival instincts become activated.

When an animal feels threatened by a predator, it doesn't have the time to think cognitively about the situation because thinking could be a waste of time that leads to death. In the face of a threat, the body instinctively kicks into gear to get the animal to safety as fast as possible. The animal's higher-level thinking shuts down, and the animal will go into fight (attack), flight (run away), or freeze (become unable to move) mode. Watch a gazelle being chased by a tiger. At first, knowing fighting will be futile, the gazelle might run away. If the gazelle is getting exhausted or sees the tiger gaining on him, the gazelle might stop running and freeze. If he's going to be eaten, freezing deadens the nerves, and the death will be less painful.

This phenomenon is the same for humans. When a person feels threatened, his fight/flight/freeze instincts turn on in order to self-protect. He will either fight (physically, verbally, or otherwise attack someone or something), flee (try to escape the situation somehow, like giving up, lying, or literally running away), or freeze (stop responding to anything). Remember, this occurs in the body, not the cognitive mind. *A person cannot think straight when he feels threatened.* He's just trying to stay alive.

That's why it often seems impossible to get any message through to the people who need it the most. Deeply into survival mode, they're not *physically, chemically* capable of listening or thinking. No matter what you say, they will not be able to process any of it whatsoever as long as they're in fight/flight/freeze. And some people who've been traumatized are *constantly* in that mode.

Now, if the gazelle doesn't get eaten and realizes the tiger is moving on his way, the gazelle will suddenly start acting funny. His movements will be jerky, jumpy. He's releasing the energy from the chase. He's completing the cycle, getting the fear of the chase out of his body. After that, the chase will not have traumatized him; it'll just be another one of his many experiences.

Humans need to do this, too. And when they don't (which happens all the time), that's when problems occur, where you'll have people who seem to always react irrationally to things in the present, but it's because they're really still reacting to a traumatic experience that happened long ago. Something in the present triggers a deep memory of the trauma and causes them to go into fight/flight/freeze mode. Oftentimes, they don't even realize it.

Healing Through the Body, Not the Mind

Humans have a right to go through major challenges and come out all right on the other end. Just because a person has been through something traumatic, that doesn't mean he has to be damaged for life. Like the gazelle, we can learn how to heal ourselves of trauma.

However, not all means of therapy adequately do the job. Most therapies deal with the cognitive mind. But trauma doesn't occur in the mind; it occurs in the body. So, as with our gazelle, it's best treated at that level: in the body.

Proper trauma therapy that takes the above into account can completely change a person's life in ways that are truly shocking. For example, during my training in trauma therapy, I learned about a man who had developed PTSD and Tourette's after his truck was blown up by a bomb. There were two other passengers in his car at the time. One of them was his best friend. Both other passengers died, while he survived, though injured.

He saw a trauma therapist who specialized in SRT (self-regulation training). Her theory was that trauma gets stuck in the physical body, and if, like the gazelle, you can work with it it physically, you can release the negative effects of the trauma. She believed that what had been diagnosed for this man as "Tourette's" was really just a failure to release the trauma from his body. She believed that the wiggling "tics" he'd developed were actually mimicking the energy of the bomb hitting his truck.

After working together, the man is now free of all symptoms of Tourette's, without medication.

If you suspect your teenager has endured trauma, I highly recommend finding a practitioner trained in SRT, which helps a person learn to recognize and respond to the physical sensations of his triggers as they arise in the body, and ultimately free himself of the trauma altogether.

There are other physical ways to deal with trauma, such as deep breathing, certain ways of singing, holding your head or putting your hand to your heart, or even sweating, tingling sensations, and yawning. You'll notice you probably naturally do some of these things when you feel startled or upset. They're done instinctively to remove the jarring experience from the body and relax the person into a state where he's capable of thinking. People unconsciously do these things because it just feels right; they're not even thinking about it. Other things that can be helpful are EMDR (eye movement desensitization and reprocessing), mindfulness exercises, and Somatic Experiencing. Sometimes medication is necessary.

The point is that a person *can* learn to go beyond his habits and intentionally release trauma in many ways. Eventually, a person can actually rewire his brain to *naturally* react differently. Whether by contacting me[6] or by reaching out to another qualified trauma therapist, please seek proper help if you know a teenager who needs it.

---

6 To learn more about my trauma therapy services, see the "About the Author" page at the end of this book for my contact information.

I love coming to these graphology sessions because I know there are things I didn't know about myself that you can help me out with. In the past four times you've been here, I realized things about myself that were getting in my way socially and kept me from being comfortable with myself.

CT, age 16

Five Highlights to Happiness

1. Own Your Own Happiness

Be responsible and independent. Seek peace inside your heart, not within your stuff, your job, or people you can't control.

2. Challenge Your Own Story

Your story is not the truth; rather, it's your perspective on the truth. You wrote the script. You can change it.

3. Make Relationships Count

With your Life Force (the One in charge), with yourself (if you don't like yourself, why should I?), and with the other people in your life. When you respect others and enjoy yourself, people want to join your party.

4. Balance Work with Play

Life isn't all about one or the other.

5. Enjoy the Journey

Celebrate all along the way, not just at the destination.

Section III

Handwriting Samples

CHAPTER 16

Seeing Is Believing

THE FOLLOWING COLLECTION of handwriting samples is from real teenagers who I've met with and counseled over the years.[7] They can be read in any order and at any time. I do encourage you to read as many as you can, because each of them is unique and offers its own invaluable insight into the real inner workings of teens.

I've included the samples for two main reasons. The first reason is to show just how useful graphology can be as a technical tool. In each sample, you will see the detailed information[8] that graphology can provide about a person. (For a list and explanations of the indicators I use, see the related addendum at the end of this book.) This can be tremendously helpful in getting to know any teen, even when you think you know everything there is to know about him...maybe *especially* if you think that. So often, we peg a teenager totally wrong. Or we don't realize the extent to which he needs help. Or we don't realize how strong a certain unmet need of his is. Understanding these things can help us and them, sometimes by giving us specific things to work on, and sometimes

---

7   Names and identifying details have been changed and/or omitted to protect privacy.

8   You might notice that the same trait in one person's handwriting might indicate something different in another person's handwriting. For example, slanted letters might mean one thing for one person and another thing for another person. This is because the whole sample is taken into account when looking at the details. The details make up the big picture, but the big picture helps define the details, as well.

by simply helping us to be more aware of their individual characteristics and thereby accept them for who they are.

The second reason is less about the technical aspects graphology has to offer and more about the stories of the teens themselves. These stories are reminders that *teenagers are people*. The fact that they're young and relatively inexperienced does not mean that what they *do* experience is irrelevant. Their experiences, though different from ours, are just as valuable, real, powerful, and important. Teens aren't too young to be taken seriously, nor is any child at any age. They're not too young to have baggage or deep issues that hold them back. You'll notice that not one of these teens is free of internal struggle of some sort. A few of those included are relatively balanced and healthy, but even they have some sort of inner challenge, and most are *really* struggling. Many of these teens seem normal on the outside but experience real abuse or some other kind of trauma that affects them at their core. Sometimes the abuse comes in the form of a school that's too dogmatic and harsh, sometimes from parents who have unrealistic expectations and are overly demanding, and sometimes it's actual physical, verbal, or sexual abuse. Sometimes the abuse is really just a perception of abuse where no true abuse actually occurred. Whatever the case, these teens—and many, many more teens out there—have experienced trauma that needs addressing, but that won't be addressed if nobody knows about it. It certainly won't be addressed if nobody even thinks to look for it.

As parents and educators who are busy and constantly multitasking, we easily fall into the trap of seeing our teens and their surface issues as things that need troubleshooting, as opposed to seeing our teens as real people with real feelings and real things going on in their lives. We absentmindedly brush off their concerns, desires, struggles, and disappointments as things they'll "get over," when oftentimes these experiences shape their identities forever, for better or for worse. Even if what they're going through is just for the moment, we owe it to our teens to really be there for them in that moment, instead of just trying to make the inconvenience go away.

They need the adults in their lives to see the truth of who they are and what they go through. I hope these samples will help you see who *your* teen truly is.

The Samples

CHAPTER 17

Michael
The Self-Defending Liar

Hockey is an amazing sport.
I love hockey because of the finess and skill that
need to be put into play it.
You have to be an expert skater to play hockey,
the edges cut, And turns need to be perfect everytime.
~~_____~~ Someone once asked me
if hockey is hard. My answer, Is hockey hard? Your on
a blade running on ice, While being chased by angry Men
with sticks. And all that while trying to put a 4.oz round
black piece of rubber ~~____~~ within 6 inches or mayb
less. Now ask yourself! Is hockey hard?

Indicator	Meaning
Horizontal lines dip downward (because he is left-handed, this is normal)	Not emotionally balanced
Some wavy lines across the page	Age-appropriate mood swings

Letters are medium size	Intelligent with balance between thinking and acting
Fast writing	Intellect
Left margin increases down the page	Standard for a lefty
Writing jams all the way into the right edge of the paper	Poor time-management skills
Excessive cross-outs	Covering up mistakes, dishonesty
Letters lean in different directions	Chaotic, insecure, self-sabotaging behavior

Analysis: Putting It Together

Michael is 15 years old. He is happy, intelligent, and active, yet insecure and not always emotionally balanced, seeing himself as okay at times and not okay at other times. He tries to control his surroundings in order to make a peaceful environment for himself. His high energy, quick intellect, and propensity toward chaos combine to create some problems for him. He likes to be in charge and do things his way, and while he creates rules for himself that make him feel more secure, other people's rules make him feel threatened. He worries that conceding to authority will jeopardize the security he's made for himself in his own way. In his mind, to compromise with an authority figure would jeopardize his security. Poor time management skills don't make things easier.

He has learned to lie to cover up his mistakes and inconsistencies, and many people in his life don't trust him as a result. They don't realize that the lies are really a symptom of a much bigger problem, that he lies to keep himself safe. While it gives him a (false) sense of security in the moment, it causes bigger problems than the original errors themselves.

Our Meeting

I told him, "I see you are a smart, take-charge person. Your primary goal is to keep yourself safe. To accomplish this, you try to make your own rules. Most adults in authority will have a hard time controlling you because of your high energy and chaotic behavior. Your rules have created a safe environment for yourself, but you still need to learn how to get along with others, especially adults and people who disagree with you."

I showed him the things he crossed out in his sample and explained that they indicate occasional lies. The lies might be about not following parents' directions, failing a test, breaking something, or any other perceived mistake. The point is that he worries what will happen if his parents, teachers, or friends find out he messed up, so he lies to protect himself. I gently told him that everyday mistakes rarely destroy relationships when handled honestly. In fact, most relationships become closer when challenges are shared openly and without judgement, even if they're not overcome. Additionally, mistakes are actually a major key to any person's growth, *if* you allow yourself to learn from them. I also pointed out the negative consequences of covering up mistakes: failure to learn important lessons from life experiences, and loss of trust, potentially even long term.

His homework:
1. Become aware when he covers up.
2. Try to understand why he feels the need to conceal.

A Pleasant Surprise

Two hours after our 30-minute session, Michael met me in the hall and thanked me for enlightening him. He told me he had just gotten off the phone with his parents. He'd apologized to them for not being honest and told them that he was determined to become a more honest person.

DID YOU KNOW?

Scientifically speaking, for a teenager and an adult to feel the same rush, the teenager needs to take a bigger risk.

CHAPTER 18

Anna
The Survivor Looking for Love

THE FIRST SAMPLE BELOW IS from when I met 14-year-old Anna at the beginning of her school year in September. Since then, we've met on a number of occasions, and I've analyzed her handwriting many of those times. I have become somewhat of a mentor to her, and we discuss her deepest fears and thoughts, oftentimes alongside her handwriting. The samples that follow are fascinating because you can clearly see and track her progress and experience through her handwriting.

From September through May, Anna was going through an all-too-familiar teenage experience: the attachment and breakup between her and an older boy. Anna was happy and content in September before she and the boy met. She met him online in October, and by November she was in love with him; she felt he understood her. By December they had parted ways (having never actually met face to face), and by January she was somewhat "over" him. In some ways, the handwriting tells the story better than I could. Let's take a look.

September

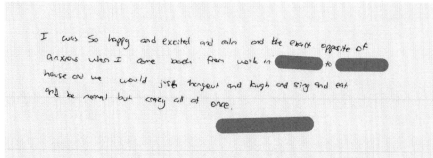

I was so happy and excited and calm and the exact opposite of anxious when I came back from work in ▇▇▇ to ▇▇▇ house and we would just hangout and laugh and sing and eat and be normal but crazy all at once.

Indicator	Meaning
Wavy lines across the page	Trying to figure out who she is, normal behavior for her age
Lines droop at ends	She is tired, probably from going to bed too late
Small letters	Intelligent, will work hard on something that interests her Quick speed Fast thinker
Perpendicular (up and down) orientation of her writing	She usually thinks before she acts
Slightly large upper margin	Pretends to like most people until she determines who is safe enough to select as a friend and then focuses on them
Large right margin	Will venture into the unknown with great care, not wanting to give the appearance of incompetence
Firm pressure	Emotionally protective of her fragile self-image
Large spaces between words	Enjoys a safe distance from people
Slightly illegible letter formation	Really good at expressing herself through writing, but thinks faster than she can speak, which inhibits communication in conversations at times
Lowercase Y's and G's are curved and open to the left in lower zone	Strong desire for approval, normal for her age

Capital I with lines above and below	Stable family life (with foster parents)
Signature appears in the right third of the page	Desire to take care of herself

Analysis: Putting It Together

Anna is a poised, intelligent, and socially capable girl. She loves learning new things and really tries to understand her environment. She understands that she controls her own destiny, which is very mature and atypical for her age. She is capable and quite good at whatever she does, but still she fears new things and what others will think of her. Her talents make her feel she is better than others, and her self-image depends on that feeling because deep down she is worried about not being good enough. She doesn't appreciate people correcting her and showing her up. She looks for approval and validation from others, hiding the fact that she doesn't know who she is. Although she is cautious with unfamiliar people and doesn't let people get too close (as a healthy defense mechanism), she does warm up more to those she feels safe with. She is quiet and thinks before she acts. She likes to be in control of her environment but doesn't want so many responsibilities that multiple levels of problems descend upon her at once. She gets angry, but she keeps it inside. Like many teens, she goes to bed too late. It appears that she has had a balanced family life, which has given her internal strength and security.

Some Background

Overall, Anna is a survivor who is trying (rather successfully) to figure out her life. She is very mature for her age, despite major challenges. Her father rarely has anything to do with her. Her mother is emotionally unstable and cannot take care of her or her many older siblings. None of her siblings has the time or ability to give Anna the care she needs. She lives with a foster family where both the mother and father truly love her.

Despite her confidence in the areas she's talented in, Anna gives the impression of being slightly sad and needy. Still, she is a delightful girl who people enjoy being around.

November

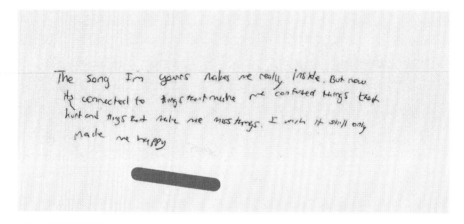

The song I'm yours makes me really inside. But now its connected to things that make me confused things that hurt and things that make me miss things. I wish it still only made me happy

Indicator	Meaning
Upper margin is much larger	Very cautious
Wavy lines across page	Increased insecurity
Lines dip farther downward at ends	Increased sadness
Signature slants steeply downward	Increased desire to be perceived as sad
Very angular letter M	Intolerant of others' viewpoints
Some Y's end with a downward movement, while some curve to the left	Wants to be left alone but seeks acknowledgement at the same time

Analysis: Putting It Together

Two months later, there's a profound difference in Anna's handwriting. Though many components remain the same, her November sample is troubling. Anna is closing herself off from the outside world. Though she is talkative, she is unsure of herself. Anna has stopped listening to others—especially adults. She'll hear them out, but she has tunnel vision and thinks she knows what to do and how to do it. She wants others to think she is sad, and this is the main way she tries to connect with others.

She has become impulsive, self-centered, and reckless. She feels confused and scared, and she'll even admit it. Still, she wants to be on her own. Her handwriting says she's spinning out of control.

What changed?

Some Background

She met a 15-year-old boy online who professed his love for her. The boy has already had two romantic relationships, and he doesn't stop talking about the last girl who broke his heart. He appears to be manipulative; in fact, Anna says she knows the boy is a jerk, but she feels they love each other. They listen to each other's problems. He gives Anna attention, emotional connection, and purpose: he wants her to help him heal his broken heart. They talk almost exclusively online and a little on the phone. They have never met face to face. Anna craves an emotional connection; she desperately desires to be needed and cared for, but she doesn't have the experience or emotional development to handle a romantic relationship. She isn't capable of understanding what's happening to her. She is at risk, and she doesn't see that she's going down a slippery slope.

When young teens date and fall in love, it is rarely logical. It's difficult if not impossible to develop a secure relationship with another person without knowing who you are and what you truly need and want. For this reason, very few teenage romances last very long. In general, teenagers between 12 and 15 do not have a developed or secure sense of self. This can be seen in the wavy writing across the page that is so typical of handwriting samples of this age group. Their awareness of their likes, dislikes, and strengths is not well defined. Their belief systems are challenged (and changing) daily. The answers to *who am I, what am I, where am I going, and what do I believe in?* are ideas that are only beginning to be formed. It is very common, even expected, that a teen could feel good about himself one moment but then confused the next, especially when he's in unfamiliar territory and has to make a decision he's never made before.

Teens aren't *physically, chemically* capable of thinking rationally at all times. Anna is getting emotionally attached, but her intellect is not developed enough to understand what she's doing. She can't self–regulate. Emotional attachment without an intellectual component is dangerous, mindless, a recipe for drama and emotional pain. While her emotions are very intense and developing rapidly, her more slowly developing intellect isn't strong enough to provide direction, stability, or restraint.

December

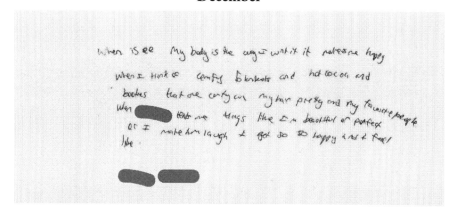

Indicator	Meaning
Large left margin	Self-doubt
Wavy lines across the page	Confusion
Lower zone of the Y loops to the left	Wants more attention
Ends of lines drop sharply downward	Not getting enough sleep
Choppy, jerky, inconsistent writing form	Broken heart
Wavy signature, like marching across the page	Insecurity but with courage

Analysis: Putting It Together

Anna is really doubting herself. She feels worried, upset, and disappointed. Her heart is torn, and she feels like a failure. She is confused, insecure, and lonely. She is, however, more open to learning from others' insights, but it's hard for her to focus. This whole episode is wearing her out, and she's exhausted. Through it all, she still has courage. We already learned from Anna's first sample that she is a survivor. She still has that in her, but she is wounded and trying to regroup.

Some Background

Anna's boyfriend dumped her for another girl in December. This sample was written soon after the breakup. In her heart, she is still attached to him.

Even weeks after the breakup, swirling thoughts kept her up at night. She questioned her womanhood, beauty, specialness, and importance. She wanted to be desired and be made to feel pretty, unique, heard, and understood.

Anna got so confused in the drama that she simply couldn't handle it. She became moody, compulsive, and unable to regulate her behavior, even when she knew better. She would call the boy on a whim, then hate herself for it. She started binge eating, then she'd exercise too much. She was short and sharp with friends, emotions running rampant. It was a full body experience. She was totally out of control.

January

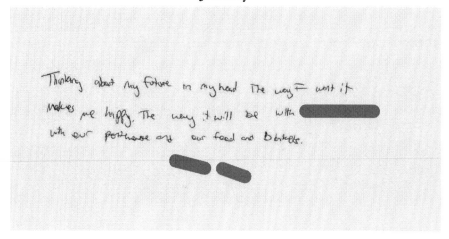

Indicator	Meaning
Return of a healthy small left margin	Less self-doubt
Lines across page still wavy	Confusion
Lines across page still dipping downward	Exhaustion
Choppy, jerky, inconsistent writing form	Broken heart
Y loops are now rounded and more open, facing the left	Open to others' opinions
Signature sinks deeply downward	Wants others to think she's sad

Analysis: Putting It Together

Anna's writing sample is beginning to look more like it did in September, though it will take more time to regain her full confidence. She's still brokenhearted and confused, but she feels more strength in her sense of self and is more willing to heed others' advice. A lot of what's shown here is not even related to the breakup but is just your regular age-appropriate stuff that any teen goes through. All teens are trying to figure out who they are, what they're doing, and what they believe. Slowly, she's getting back to normal.

The really interesting thing here is that Anna's signature indicates sadness or depression, while the rest of her handwriting sample only indicates some insecurity, *not* sadness or depression. She is acting. Why?

Background

The boy fooled her. She discovered that he had been two-timing her. Finally, Anna realized the boy wasn't treating her nicely. She is so embarrassed at being fooled, and she is actually more upset by that than by the breakup itself. She gives herself a pity party so that others will give her the sympathy she needs. She's not thinking straight. She has a lot to process.

Anna was totally addicted to controlling her environment. When she got herself into a relationship she couldn't control, she felt so overwhelmed that she became something she never thought she'd become: a victim. This girl had already been through a lot in her young life, and she'd always risen above everything, until now. Why all of a sudden would she fall apart? Through all her challenges, she'd overcome them all by controlling her environment. But now that someone else controlled *her,* she lost her equilibrium and didn't know what to do. She was lost. Simply put, she just needed sympathy for once, now that she couldn't be there for herself in the way she was used to.

This sample is a stark example of the effects of teenage dating drama. Just like after an illness, she will need time to heal. How she chooses to frame her experiences and her attitude going forward will make all the difference in her new outlook on life.

May

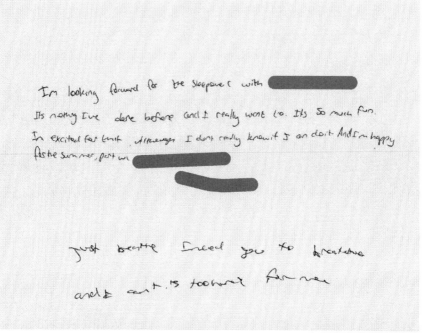

Indicator	Meaning
Left and right margins appropriate size	Good sense of balance between herself and others
Wavy lines across page	Unsettled (age appropriate)
Upper margin wider than before	Increased cautiousness with new people
Left margin decreases down the page	Cautiousness
Spacing between words, not too far apart or too close, same as in September	Confidence, gaining more control
Legible writing	Increased communication skills
Writing style is both angular and rounded	Angular: dogmatic Rounded: emotional, talkative
Clarity diminishes and spacing increases under duress	Communication skills diminish under stress

Analysis: Putting It Together

It is now eight months since Anna's first sample. We are finally seeing a renewed sense of confidence. Her new knowledge and experiences, though difficult, have helped her come more into herself and return to her survivor's outlook on life. She is more stable. She's happier and still personable but now more cautious. Her goal is to control her surroundings with her intellect. She observes her environment like radar, constantly scanning, always on alert. She interviews people and isn't as quick to accept them as before. Anna is trying very hard to maximize her nature and nurture to keep herself safe, meaning, she is trying to be true to herself while being real about the world around her.

Anna needs more time to energize, organize, and keep herself safe. She likes her privacy but also enjoys communicating and socializing with others. She is looking for approval, acceptance, and camaraderie from others, which is typical behavior for her age. Feedback from others helps teens learn socially acceptable standards, morality, and more. She does not communicate well under pressure, and she seeks privacy to understand her new stressful situation. Drama, i.e., stress and her reactions to it, will cause her to regroup, re-educate, reorganize, and rededicate.

Her signature suggests she wants others to believe she is vulnerable. This seeming vulnerability is only a defense mechanism to protect her from other people's expectations of her. She thinks others expect her to always be on top of her game, and she's scared she won't measure up. This behavior is her story about herself.

Background

How can you learn from the past if you don't understand or even know what happened? A 14-year-old can only grasp so much about her roller coaster of emotions, feelings of being taken advantage of, and loss of personal control.

Just like a five-year-old cannot pick up 100 pounds, a 14-year-old's brain is not developed enough to have a fully rational outlook on life. It's just nature. Anna will hopefully understand more as she matures and gets older. Until then, only so much can be expected of her.

In May, Anna said, "I got a handle on this." Her solution: "I'll look for another boyfriend." She got into multiple relationships that were not solid. She's starting to realize that relationships are not where it's at for her right now, but as a 14-year-old, the thrill is in the risky behavior. Anna wants to figure out boys, drinking, drugs. She wants to stay up late. She confidently believes that she is in control, that she will get through anything that comes her way. Anna thinks she's okay now.

Survivors have hope.

DID YOU KNOW?

On average, teens spend nine hours online daily (yes, you read that right!), and 70 percent hide their online activity from their parents.

CHAPTER 19

Dan

The Abuse Victim with Red Flags

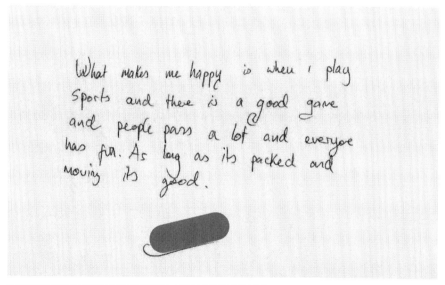

What makes me happy is when I play sports and there is a good game and people pass a lot and everyone has fun. As long as its packed and moving its good.

Indicator	Meaning
Felon claw Y and G	Sexual trauma, probably regularly and at a young age
Large lower zones that interfere with next line	Stress
Double loops	Self-protection
Inconsistent slants	Insecurities
Extra long spaces between words	Very distant from others

Large left margin	Strong sense of not being good enough
Large right margin	Doesn't like to take initiative
Rivers	Hears opinions as criticisms, doesn't like to let people in
Clear writing	Good communicator
Medium sized writing	Balance of thought with action
Sample is framed in the middle of the page	Cautious
Large underlined signature	Life of the party

Analysis: Putting It Together

There are major red flags here. This 18-year-old boy has deep secrets that he does not share. He is very private and wants to maintain control. He has been deeply hurt and has built many defenses to protect his wounds from exposure. While I cannot tell what all of these secrets are, I can see that he has endured some kind of sexual abuse.

But, like all of us, he is multifaceted. He is a good communicator who balances thought with action. He likes to be the life of the party. He is interesting to talk to and fun to spend time with. Despite his social side, he likes to stay impersonal. He does not like people getting into his business, which he perceives as attempts to control him.

Dan is subconsciously expressing: "See me, have fun with me, but don't get too close because I fear my secrets will be exposed and you won't like me. I'll sabotage any attempt at closeness to protect myself. I've been hurt enough, and I don't want to be hurt again."

Our Meeting

Why Dan came to a graphologist is a mystery to me. Sometimes people like him want to be discovered and helped. At other times, they think nobody can understand them, and they want to prove it. I want to ascertain what he hopes to gain from the session.

He is very private and does not share his feelings easily. I respect this and start by saying, "If I am going into an area of your life where you don't want me to be, just tell me, and I will stop immediately."

I explain that the purpose of this analysis is to gain a vocabulary and a voice to see oneself in a new, different light. The more I share with him, the more comfortable he becomes.

I start by telling him that he likes to be the life of the party, that people enjoy being around him. However, he doesn't want people getting too close, offering their opinions of him, or trying to tell him what to do.

I gauge his reaction to determine whether I should tell him more details about his sample. I tell him that nobody else has power over him, and nobody's opinion about him matters unless he decides it does. I might even go so far as to say that while we can't control what other people do to us, we can control how we choose to feel about it (even though it might be very difficult), and we can choose how to move forward. I hope that these ideas might offer him a baby step toward finding his own peace, but he might not even want to hear that.

Next, I point out the felon claws in his sample and explain they indicate a major emotional event in the past. I do not get more specific than that, and I stress that I do not need to know the details. I emphasize the importance of being guided by a wise person, someone who can teach him how to use his past to strengthen his present.

A felon-claw writer very much needs outside intervention. Their predators used pain, guilt, shame, and isolation to control them. Even years later, victims feel distant, dirty, and unlovable. They often feel unworthy of close relationships, or even of being liked at all. They believe they have significant character flaws that prevent others from connecting with them. They fear that others will eventually find out that they are flawed and despicable. My goal is to inspire him to see a professional who specializes in trauma. With time, patience, and proper professional help, Dan can heal.

Chapter 20

Brad
The Good Student
Who Needed More Ego

I have lived in ▓▓▓▓▓ all my life and I enjoy it very much. I have a great passion ~~come~~ for ~~firearms~~ firearms and have build many myself. I also enjoy training people to use them. I hope to be able to make a living from this when I get older.

I enjoy making and building firearms. I have many choices in building these things. I love the AR15.

Indicator	Meaning
Clear writing	Good communicator
Evenly spaced	Interpersonal relationships come easily
Quick speed	Intelligent
Small script	Detail oriented
Mistakes are crossed out by a single line	Accepts own imperfections

Lines travel across the page on an overly exaggerated upward slant	Hides negative feelings
Wavy lines	Trying to figure out where he wants to go
Inconsistent writing	Insecure
Signature begins 60 percent of the way toward the right margin	Likes to be in charge
Last two quickly written lines are jagged and less readable	Becomes dogmatic and loses some of his ability to communicate under pressure

Analysis: Putting It Together

Brad, age 19, is an excellent student and very skilled communicator. He's confident, smart, and unafraid of hard work. He has a strong desire to do well and is aware of his strengths. At the same time, he is confused, ashamed, and disappointed with his life, yet he fakes being happy. Why?

Background

The virtue of humility was impressed upon him very strongly. Because he is a sincere person who really tries his best in life, he wanted to be as humble as possible. He mistakenly took this to a false extreme where feeling good about himself at all meant having an inflated ego. So every time he felt any satisfaction from his achievements (which, thanks to his skills, talents, and work ethic, were numerous), he thought he wasn't humble, which made him depressed, which made him feel stressed and empty, which made him think something was wrong with him. He thought striving for humility would bring him joy. He wondered why, after all his efforts toward trying to be a good, confident, humble, straightforward adult, it wasn't working out so well. He was embarrassed and confused. So he faked that he was happy, all the while suffering quietly. He was disappointed with himself, with his life, and with his faith. Brad was lost and needed to talk to someone.

Our Meeting

The main thing we discussed was the big question of how a person is supposed to feel good about himself and still be humble. It seems to be a contradiction. His major misunderstanding was thinking that he needed to eradicate his ego entirely. Brad was so busy making himself into a nothing that there was nothing left to make humble.

He was too ashamed to discuss this with anyone. Had I not seen it in his handwriting and pointed it out, he wouldn't have opened up about it. This is true of many teens with varying issues. The discovery was the catalyst that enabled his healing to begin.

Once Brad becomes comfortable developing and respecting his ego, he will feel more in touch, calm, and happy in his daily life.

Chapter 21

Lauren
The Girl with Social Anxiety

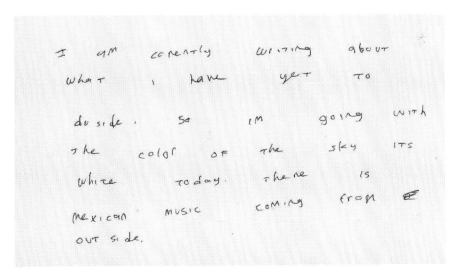

Indicator	Meaning
Paragraph aesthetically placed on the page	Pleasant personality, dresses nicely, appreciates quality
Good form (not rigid or unruly)	Generally happy and self-accepting
Pressure is light	Sensitive
Substantial spacing between each word	Needs a lot of distance from people to re-energize
Each letter and word rises upward	Strong desire to appear happy in social situations

Small capital letters	Feels inferior
Small personal pronoun I	Feels inferior
Excessive cross-out	Covering up mistakes

Analysis: Putting It Together

This very sensitive 16-year-old girl is very cautious about putting herself in situations that might cause her pain. She needs a lot of time to herself. Though there's nothing abnormal about needing alone time, or even preferring it to interacting with others, the writer's extreme desire to disconnect from people points to social fears and anxiety. Somewhere in Lauren's past, she was probably hurt (cannot be determined from this sample). She does not trust people but has a strong desire to appear happy in social situations. This gives her stress around others, making it difficult to act in accordance with social norms and causing her to feel inferior. She worries about what people think of her. All the social stress makes her sad and afraid.

Despite her challenges, she largely accepts herself for who she is. Her overall attitude: "Well, that's me." She seems to be able to interact well in small circles when she feels in control. She's intelligent and generally happy. In fact, she enjoys the pleasure of her own company, and she occupies her free time wisely.

Background

When you meet Lauren, she smiles and seems happy. But the smile doesn't tell the whole story. Even with people she knows, she sits in the back corner so she can watch everyone and be less vulnerable to them. She understands that it's not logical, but her defense mechanisms come up and make her feel that she needs to protect herself. Her classmates and teachers are friendly and respectful, but she still doesn't trust them. When I'd tease her saying, "They're vicious girls!" she'd laugh and say, "I know it's not rational."

So what is Lauren afraid of? She's afraid of a memory. I point out to her that in her 20-person class, there *might* be one person who could bother her. Lauren's strategy is to be afraid of all 20 for fear of that one person. This fear prevents her from actually seeing and listening to other people and ascertaining who they really are.

Even with these struggles, Lauren is otherwise a healthy teenage girl. She very much treats herself as her own best friend. She accepts herself. She likes to read, write, draw, and do yoga, and she entertains herself for long periods of time. She eats and sleeps properly, and she doesn't deprive herself.

She does have a good friend or two, but she is also happy spending time alone. It doesn't bother or depress her to spend time with only herself. The only loneliness she experiences is in a group with lots of people. Even then, she doesn't berate herself for feeling that way; she just accepts that this is how she feels. This shows amazing maturity on her part.

There's an important lesson here. Some parents would be going nuts trying to get a daughter like Lauren to be more social. Making a big deal out of her social issues will cause Lauren more insecurity and make the problem persist even more. Of course, Lauren would readily admit that she would rather not feel uncomfortable in groups of people, but she is also very stable and content in her life, even with this challenge. Parents often think something's wrong with their child if the child isn't highly social. This just isn't true. While some people are more social, just as many aren't, and both are totally normal and fine. Being a loner isn't a problem in and of itself. Lauren does have relationships with others. She also has a really solid relationship with herself. As a parent, there's no reason to push teens like Lauren to be social when they don't want to. If she wants help with the anxiety part, then great, but the social aspect alone isn't a true problem.

CHAPTER 22

Andy
The Boy Who Didn't Star
In His Own Movie

The school I go to is called ▬▬▬▬▬
In school I learn many subjects. School starts at around 9
o'clock but I have to be in the building by 7:30 because that's
when Davening starts.

Indicator	Meaning
Poor use of right margin	Poor time management skills
Wavy written line across page	Unsure of himself
Capital I written like a number 2	Feels second in his own life
Large spaces between words	Needs time to himself to recharge
Rivers	Not open to others' opinions
Quick writing	Intelligent
Small writing	Gets involved in details
Unstable pitch	Insecure
Clear writing	Good communicator
Writing not angular	Easygoing, not dogmatic, likes peace

Analysis: Putting It Together

Andy is a great guy. He is easygoing and has a pleasant disposition. He doesn't get worked up in social situations and likes a peaceful environment. He likes to engage with others but needs time to himself to recharge. He is extremely intelligent and is an excellent communicator, but he doesn't feel a need to rub it in anyone's face or prove anything to anyone.

Despite impressive strengths and talents, Andy is unsure of himself. He doesn't feel like the star of his own movie. He doesn't feel good enough for that status and thinks there's something wrong with him. I call a kid like this an "OWE," which stands for "Own Worst Enemy." This begins at an early age. OWEs consistently fail to see themselves as good enough, even though they are above average in many areas. Andy's insecurities make Andy get in his own way. He is afraid to take charge of his life and be a star.

Why would someone who is smart, friendly, and talented feel so insecure?

Parents tell their kids they love them all equally, that they don't compare one to the other, and that they accept them no matter what. Teachers tell their students that everyone is unique. Often these messages don't stick. Why? Because parents and teachers often *do* seem to prefer some kids more than others. An adult can say whatever he wants, but talk is cheap if it's not followed up by actions that reinforce the message. Children hear and detect comparisons. They learn that people do judge.

We don't know for certain whether this is why Andy has such a distorted view of himself. We do know that his environment can cause his self-worth to crumble. Parents and teachers with teens like Andy (with any teen or child, for that matter): take extra care of your words and actions to make sure that your children don't have a reason to second guess your feelings for them or your opinion of them. At the same time, Andy needs to be taught that his value is not dependent on others (not even on his parents and teachers). (See previous section entitled "Your Life Force Makes You Great" for more on this.)

CHAPTER 23

Lyle
The Abuse Victim
Who Needed Chaos

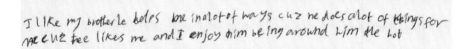

Indicator	Meaning
No upper margin	Lack of trust in others, observes to determine who is safe
Edge-to-edge writing (no right or left margin)	Doesn't want to hear others' opinions
Angular writing	Nervousness
Blotchiness, very slow writing	Exceptionally cautious
Chaotic writing	Trying to control environment through chaos
Close spacing between words	Very social

Signature far in left corner	Likes to be directed, doesn't like responsibility
Fast writing slightly bigger	Works better under pressure
Letters' sizes are inconsistent	Insecurity
Fast writing looks nearly the same as normal-speed writing	Always under duress

Analysis: Putting It Together

Lyle is a nervous, edgy, and chaotic 13-year-old boy. He does not trust other people, and he isn't sure of himself, either. He does not want people to get to know him. He likes to be part of a group and will conform to it once he trusts them, but he becomes silent when in a new group of people, observing and judging them to determine who he thinks he can trust. Still, he wants to think for himself. He sets up a barrier between himself and people in positions of authority.

Lyle was abused. It's unclear what kind of abuse he suffered, but it's abundantly clear that he's in tremendous pain. He is stressed all the time, in a constant state of fight or flight, without a moment of reprieve. He can't stay still or think clearly. He's all over the place, creating chaos wherever he goes. Chaos and stress are his comfort zone; he's actually more open and aware of his surroundings under pressure. So, in creating this chaos, he is controlling an environment full of unknowns and perceived possible threats.

He's smart and creative, and he loves to get into the details when he's interested in something. Unfortunately, his cognitive abilities are diminished because his abuse has made him feel constantly in danger.

Lyle's daily challenges are harder for him than they would be for other kids. On top of it, he makes things difficult for himself. But he doesn't give up. Even though his efforts are not extremely successful, he's tenacious, he perseveres. He is determined to be in charge of himself and to overcome obstacles.

Background

People who are abused often feel they lost their power and have a strong desire to maintain control. At only thirteen years old, Lyle has a very limited ability to grasp the true concept of his power. What he knows is that he was hurt, and the adults in his life couldn't—or didn't—protect him. His logic is that the more chaos he creates around him, the more power and control he will have, and the more he'll be able to protect himself.

So he gets into trouble. He lies, he calls out in class, he bothers the kid in front of him when he's bored, he walks out of class without permission, he'll take a half-hour bathroom break. He does not listen, and when he gets bored or insecure, his creative mind looks for excitement. He has trouble following the rules because he doesn't want to follow *their* rules. *He's* in control. Nobody's going to tell him what to do, and nobody can punish him into compliance. The consequences of his behaviors are small prices to pay for safety.

The only way to help Lyle is to gain his confidence and trust. Using graphology can help. Describing what the handwriting shows about Lyle's experience and personality can show him that he's understood. It's a beginning.

So we talked about all this. We discussed the fact that it's normal to have a hard time following rules, but that doesn't make it acceptable behavior. It is normal that he has a strong drive for excitement and adventure. It is also normal that he sometimes makes poor decisions based on feelings instead of logic. It is important for a teen to feel normal when doing normal things. At the same time, part of the challenge of growing up is learning what actions are appropriate at what times.

He needs to know that his lying and sneakiness cause adults not to trust him, and that there are real-life consequences for acting so erratically. But these talks need to be enveloped in kindness, and the lessons need to be repeated continuously. Though he is limited by his own nature, he can learn to change with constant, loving guidance, as well as through deep breathing exercises, thinking critically about his behaviors during times of calm, and also just through getting older. We can only expect so much given his age and circumstances.

His biggest stumbling block is his trauma. All teens have trouble thinking logically. A teen who has been abused has an additional struggle with logic because the abuse has made him feel constantly in danger, and a perceived threat turns the primitive survival brain on and turns the rational brain off. He has to deal with his abuse before his brain will be able to function in a healthy way. I suggested that he do some trauma therapy, which would hopefully get him out of threat mode and into healing mode.

DID YOU KNOW?

Comparing teenagers with adults, teenagers experience more pleasure from the same reward.

CHAPTER 24

Jarrod
The Boy Who Needed
A Physical Outlet

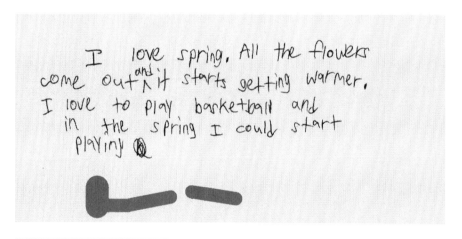

I love spring. All the flowers
come out and it starts getting warmer.
I love to play barketball and
in the spring I could start
playing

Indicator	Meaning
Wavy line across the page	Poor self-image
Individual words lean left on the left side of the line and right on the right side	Has trouble following routines
Weak lower zone and some G's and Y's too open to the left	Looking for acceptance, inability to express or access emotions
Angles inside rounded letters (P in play)	Suppressed anger

Lowercase A's are springboards	Trying to run away from others, doesn't want to be seen
Retracing letters	Mistrust of self and others
Excessive cross-outs	Excessive concern about his mistakes
Thick, grinding period punctuation	Anger
Heavy pressure	Puts up a wall for protection
Large right margin	Fear of new things

Analysis: Putting It Together

Jarrod is a bright and energetic 13-year-old boy, but his intense anxiety and sorely lacking confidence make his life very hard. He is full of physical energy that, because of his age, is not matched with equal cognitive awareness or ability, so he quickly acts without thinking, often regretting his actions later. He doesn't know where his place in the universe is and doesn't have any idea what he's doing.

All of this makes it exceedingly difficult for him to relate to and communicate with others. He is so worried about what others will think and how they will respond that he doesn't have a clue of what to say or do in almost any situation. He wants to be firm and have people take him seriously, but his lacking confidence compels him to keep trying out different personalities, or to show off, which annoys people.

He calls out in class because he wants to prove that he knows something, then he gets punished for it. The other kids make fun of him for it, so he hits someone. Then he gets kicked out of class. He doesn't want to get kicked out of class. He'll play a game and then he wont play it; he'll hog the ball at recess trying to look like a star, but he looks like a fool. He doesn't know what to do with himself.

It is a challenge for Jarrod to concentrate on anything for any length of time, and he has trouble following routines. He has a constant inner battle between his nature and his desire to conform to social norms. He works hard to do his best and gets upset when he doesn't meet others' expectations. He feels he's not good enough and can't win.

Adults interacting with Jarrod might easily label him as a "bad kid." He's not a bad kid, but that label could turn him into one, as happens with so many kids who are just trying to get by as best they can.

Even though his actions warrant punishment, that doesn't negate his need for love and understanding. He desperately needs kindness and stability with his discipline (as does every child and teenager). Care and understanding will go a long way. He is young, and his ability to think cognitively will grow. Time and safe, understanding adults can help him mature. Jarrod is just confused and needs guidance to help him come into himself.

Playing sports or getting into some kind of regular intense exercise is often a great and easy solution for kids like Jarrod. He desperately needs somewhere to channel his abundance of physical energy so that it doesn't come out in areas that cause him problems. Additionally, such an outlet can improve his focus, as well as give him an opportunity to learn a skill and build confidence in something he might be good at. Whether it's joining a basketball team or just going for a daily run by himself, it really doesn't matter. He can pick whatever appeals to him. As they say, a tired boy is a healthy boy.

DID YOU KNOW?

Sick of your teenager's sleep habits?

Cut him some slack. Because of their natural circadian rhythms, teens' bodies are wired to go to bed late and wake up late, and they need 9-10 hours of sleep a night. However, most teens don't get nearly that amount, due to school starting early, heavily demanding schedules and homework, and excessive phone/internet usage.

Teen sleep deprivation (technically less than 7.3 hours nightly) is extremely common and is associated with cognitive impairment, moodiness, anxiety, and depression.

CHAPTER 25

Brooke
The Girl Nobody Knew Was Suffering

September

On Succos my grandparents from ▮▮▮▮ came,
They slept in my room and I had to sleep upstairs
with my sisters in one room. It wasn't so fun.
but It was great to have them in our house.

Indicator	Meaning
Large upper margin	Feels unsafe
Large left margin	Feels not good enough
Rising lines across the page	Faking happiness
Lower zone interferes with next line's upper zone	Stress
Slant of letters is inconsistent	Insecurity
Creative strokes	Creative and intelligent
Line crosses out signature	Self-sabotage, despair, and loneliness

Analysis: Putting It Together

In this September sample, this extremely stressed 14-year-old girl is two weeks into a new school year at a new school. She tries to give the impression of being happy, bubbly, and upbeat. She pretends to be carefree, hiding her sadness, nervousness, and feelings of failure with a smile. She is a secretive, frustrated person who tries to make herself bigger than she is but then sabotages herself. Deep in a pit of despair and loneliness, she feels she is not enough.

Background

Not long before the above sample was written at the beginning of her ninth grade year, Brooke was in a different school where she struggled in just about every area. She had a hard time making friends and was a C and D student to boot.

Throughout eighth grade, Brooke got into a lot of minor problems in her old school. Her detention folder was thick. The school disciplined her and other students with what I call "school abuse," unfair punishments with neither true teaching value nor care for or insight into the student as a human being. To make matters worse, the students had no interaction with the principal or anyone else who they could speak to about problems they were having with the teachers.

After eighth grade, Brooke went to a different, more progressive high school. The staff was made aware that Brooke had a lot of potential but was suffering from the shock of school abuse. The above sample is from the beginning of the year at this new school, whereas the following sample is from the end of that year.

May

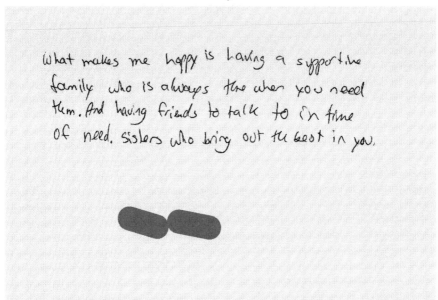

Indicator	Meaning
Average size upper and left margin	Emotionally balanced
Large right margin	Fear of duplicating her success
Wavy lines across the page	Insecurity
Lines and words nicely spaced	Socially comfortable
Legible writing	Communicates well
Uneven slant of letters	Insecurity
Loops in the lower zone	Desire for feedback from others
Signature dips downward across the page	Feigning sadness for attention

Analysis: Putting It Together

At the end of the school year eight months later, Brooke's writing shows a very different girl with a lot of personal growth. Brooke is now much more relaxed with herself and others. She is loved and accepted by her teachers and other students, and she even has three or four good friends. She gets A's and B's and doesn't get into trouble anymore. On the surface, she seems to be a happy and a well-adjusted student.

The pain from her previous school's abuse is still present, and her old memory patterns remain; this will take time to change. Even though she's capable, she doesn't see herself that way. She fears that her new successes might be temporary and that she'll revert to her old self. This fear is normal for any teen, especially someone in Brooke's shoes. Not entirely comfortable with herself, she feels like a victim. She has high expectations for herself, but she expresses herself in a lower fashion so that others won't expect too much of her. She hides her pride so that nobody can take away her dignity.

At the same time, she has a strong desire for feedback from others. A teenager of fourteen or fifteen has rarely developed the internal strength required for learning to have a positive attitude. This is why the adults in her life play such a pivotal role for giving her what she's not yet able to give herself. Seeing herself positively through others' eyes helps Brooke learn to trust herself and to truly believe that she is all right. As she gets older, and hopefully spends more time in a nurturing environment, she'll begin to see herself differently. However, she *does* already feel significantly better about herself, and her new accomplishments are astounding compared to the previous year. The new school has clearly been excellent for her.

I showed Brooke the difference in her handwriting so that she could see her own growth. The visual of comparing these two very different samples was a powerful component in getting Brooke to believe in herself. Seeing tangibly that she *has* truly changed increased her confidence and self-image, and it has helped her believe that she could indeed go on to do even more and better. Seeing is believing.

Really, most of what I'm doing is planting seeds. Though Brooke might not understand everything I say right away, it might hit her a couple years later. Despite a probably incomplete understanding at present, it might not be possible for her to grasp these concepts in two years, for example, if she doesn't hear them now. I often get calls and emails from teens who I'd met years before, saying that, though they didn't understand what I was talking about when we originally met, all of a sudden they realized the truth of it all years later and started to turn their lives around as a result.

There are two main reasons this handwriting sample is important. The first one is to demonstrate what dramatic change can occur when a teen's needs are met. People assume that teens' moods, motivations, and general ways of being are just who they are for the moment and that there's nothing to be done about it. People assume teens can't change. **The reality is that when a person of any age has all his needs met (this includes emotional needs, too), he will naturally be happy, motivated, and easy to be around.** If a girl like Brooke who didn't have all her needs met suddenly gets what she needs, she can be *very* capable of change, and she can do it surprisingly quickly. This speed is partially because teens aren't jaded like so many adults, so they are more open to new paradigms once they see that their old ones weren't true. It's also partially because teens' brains are changing so fast and they're developing new skills and awarenesses every day.

Brooke is yet another one of many teens who was mislabeled as a "bad kid" because she was in a school with a messed up system of teachers and principals who had no clue what they were doing and in the meantime were breaking kids apart and unwittingly changing their lives for the worse, possibly long-term. Brooke was lucky to have switched paths to her new school, where the staff knew how to nurture kids instead of just blindly punishing them.

That being said, as parents and educators, it's important to not expect too much change overnight. We have to make a point to appreciate our teens' changes for what they are. Brooke made a dramatic change in a short period of time, but not every teen will change so quickly. If the people in those teens' lives are only satisfied with a complete turnaround, then they won't be present for the incredible change their teens *are* making in whatever amount of time it takes them. Even if a teen's circumstances change in a major way (such as switching to a different school), it can take time for the teen's feelings and behaviors to catch up.

The second reason this handwriting sample is so important is to demonstrate the tremendous impact a school has on its students. It is a given for many parents that their children will go to whatever school is closest, or whatever school a child's siblings went to, etc. This can be a huge problem. Not every school is right for every student, and sending a student to the wrong school can cause that student lifelong negative effects. Sometimes we're talking about a decent school that just isn't a good fit for everyone, and sometimes we're talking about a school that has major problems, but it doesn't occur to anyone that anything could be different, so they just sit with the problem without ever thinking of doing something about it, or even realizing it's a problem in the first place.

For example, let's say a 14-year-old girl hates the school lunches. She has some money, so she leaves school during lunch time to go get pizza. She knows it's against the rules, but she's hungry. They notice she's not there, so she's sent to the principal's office, where she's suspended for a day. Is suspension the proper way to handle this? It might be a common solution in such a situation, but that doesn't mean it's effective or appropriate. It might be the first time this girl has ever made such a decision, or ever even had the opportunity to make such a decision at this point in her young life and stage in her brain development. Instead of simply punishing her, explain the consequences of her actions, and empathize with her by relating that you understand she was hungry and that it's not easy to stick around for a lunch that she doesn't want when an alternative is right around the corner. Then ask the student, how could the problem be solved in the future? Maybe she needs to bring a better lunch from home. Maybe once a week the school gets pizza for everyone. Suspending a student for something like this just shows punishment. It teaches nothing. And guess what? Plenty of kids don't care if they miss school, and they don't necessarily even *want* to be there in the first place, so the punishment is meaningless. So often, parents and educators forget that to discipline means to teach!

When Brooke was in her old school, a school that all her friends and neighbors and siblings went to, she was suffering tremendously. Thankfully, her parents realized she needed something else, and she was able to get what she needed in a place that was more appropriate for her. But what would have happened to her had she stayed in the old school? It might have been devastating for her, maybe even forever.

The point is, don't send your kids somewhere just because it's a school. Make sure it's the right fit for your teen. If you're an educator, make sure you're offering learning opportunities and understanding for your students' mistakes instead of just punishment.

DID YOU KNOW?

More than 70 percent of girls ages 15-17 avoid leaving home (even to go to school) if they don't like the way they look.

Three out of four girls with low self-esteem (compared to one in four girls with high self-esteem) engage in destructive behavior like drinking, smoking, intentionally hurting themselves, bullying, or eating disorders.

CHAPTER 26

Mark
The Class Clown
Who Turned It Around

Age 14

I like skateboarding. I can't do any tricks. I like to relax with friends. I ... like to make people laugh.

Indicator	Meaning
Edge-to-edge writing	Doesn't allow others to get close
Many cover strokes/retracing	Mistrust of self and others
Double loops in the middle zone	Need for protection due to abuse
Excessive cross-outs	Hides mistakes
Heavy pressure	Won't let others see his vulnerability
Lines dip downward	Sadness
Letters lean both left and right	Insecurity

Left-leaning personal pronoun I	Poor self-image
Predominantly right-leaning words	Trying to be friendly
Lacking upper margin	Doesn't open up to others

Analysis: Putting It Together

Mark is a sad, angry, troubled, insecure, and lonely 14-year-old boy. Early in his life, he suffered some kind of abuse at the hands of his very dysfunctional parents, resulting for Mark in anxiety and an inability to connect with others. Not trusting most people and worrying about what others think of him, he prevents others from getting too close in case they hurt him or judge him negatively. He is friendly but on guard, determined not to open up. He worries about his inability to relate to others, but he isn't really aware that he's pushing them away. He wants to connect and belong, but he thinks nobody will like him. The strong wall he's built between himself and the outside world is a protection for his sensitive inner self.

Mark has a thin threshold when it comes to feeling unsafe, and he is not aware that he's paranoid and overreacts. He wants to be in control and thinks he can handle his life by himself. Whatever it takes for him to defend himself, he will do.

As a student, Mark is out of control. Educating him is hard. He has learning challenges and struggles to listen, focus, be still, and absorb information. He needs to understand and internalize what is being taught, but this demands a certain degree of humility, openness, and trust, which is hard for Mark. He feels constricted by the classroom's defined spaces and rules. Thinking he can fool others and distract them from his insecurities, Mark sits in the back and disrupts the class.

For someone who wants to help Mark, gaining his trust is difficult, which makes it hard for him to listen to anything and learn. It has to be a process. The best thing to do in the beginning is to build and maintain a friendship. With Mark and a lot of other teens I talk to, my friendship portal is sports talk. This is great for Mark, who wants nothing in life but to play basketball. After the friendship is solid, role-playing is a good option to help Mark understand important lessons when the opportunity arises. It allows him to experience another way of behaving that could improve future situations.

Using graphology from the beginning, a therapist or mentor (though someone like Mark really does need a therapist) can quickly understand what Mark is feeling. It is not necessary to tell Mark everything I see; the key points are enough. The rest are aids for the therapist to help understand and guide Mark. I share with Mark his dichotomy about wanting to be in friendships but not trusting others. To show someone like Mark that you have his back takes a long time. Compassion is the guiding light. Eventually, he slowly began to trust.

Age 16

Indicator	Meaning
Heavy pressure	Hiding vulnerabilities
Blobs	Covering up mistakes
Left margin increases down the page	Impulsive, has trouble tolerating others

Double loops in the middle zone	Protection from pain, from the outside world
Retracing	Mistrust of self and others
Left-leaning personal pronoun I	Poor self-image
Wavy line across the page	Insecurity
Garlands or school type M's and N's	Peaceful, likes to follow rules
Upper and lower zones touching middle zone	Emotional and intellectual distress, narcissism
Quick writing	Intelligent

Analysis: Putting It Together

Two years later, Mark has grown up and matured. He is taking more care of his responsibilities; he stays in class, doesn't clown around anymore, focuses on his tasks, and generally acts more like an appropriately behaved student. He's less defensive and paranoid around others, and he's more able to interact successfully. Though he finds it hard to trust others, he has become more open and willing to listen. This change is a significant breakthrough in his interpersonal relationships. Being hopeful is one of his great assets, and he isn't giving up. Behind the false front, Mark is an intelligent, energetic boy who just wants peace, quiet, and respect.

Mark's attitude is getting better. He had been choosing to be angry at everyone who came his way. Now he's begun to relax, function, and experience happiness. That was his choice. We are in control of our attitude about ourselves. He now actively chooses not to get upset when things don't go his way.

However, he is still burdened by his past and frustrated by his fear of trusting others. He employs defense mechanisms to keep himself safe, like being sneaky and deceitful. He will say any lie if he thinks it'll make a positive impression. Though he's improving, his narcissistic tendencies and emotional and intellectual frustrations make it very hard for Mark to play, work, or study with others. He struggles to tolerate others' differences. Despite his very real improvements, he is still deeply frustrated, confused, and unhappy.

Mark needs to know that others care for him. Putting Mark in a kind, fair, and honest environment will also help him learn to trust. For this reason, Mark is very fortunate to be in a school that's willing to stick with him, despite the difficulty he presents. Disciplining Mark with kindness and praising him for the little positive things contribute to creating a safe environment for him where he can relax, learn, and grow.

Age 19

Indicator	Meaning
Normal margins on the left and right	Good sense of self
Heavy pressure	Hiding vulnerabilities
Letters lean heavily to the right	Overly friendly
Vertical personal pronoun I	Independence
Some violation of lower zone into next line	Frustration
Large loops in the lower and upper zones	Doesn't know how to control emotions

Analysis: Putting It Together

Mark is healthier than when we first met him. The effects of abuse on Mark's attitude about himself have subsided considerably. The now-19-year-old has become a passionate and confident young man. He is more trusting and open, and he's a better listener and student. His social skills have dramatically improved, though he's a bit of a loner who values his privacy. He still longs for true emotional closeness, but he's learning how to develop it by sharing ideas and feelings. Instead of investing his time and energy into anxiety and worrying about what others think, he now invests in his own growth. He has taken the guidance from others and grown positively, changing his attitude from the inside out. Mark has worked very hard.

Interestingly, Mark has taken to fantasy/daydreaming as a healthier means of escape. It's his defense, wanting to believe in how things could be instead of how they are. He'd love to play professional sports (though he's not kidding himself), so imagining it is his way of dealing with unpleasant moments.

There are two main takeaways from Mark's story. The first takeaway: Nobody is doomed to any certain fate. Someone might start out at a low place, but he can rise up. At 14, Mark's past dominated and defined him. At 19, Mark is taking charge of his life, and his past is only a springboard for his future. Some of this change occurred simply as a gift of time and biological/chemical development, while some of it was more than that.

The second: It takes a community to help any teen mature. If someone's in a hostile environment with one person who's nice to him, that one person would be a safe haven, but the environment as a whole would likely make him feel generally unsafe. There are a lot of people in any person's life, and every person has an effect. Yes, Mark had to make the choice to turn his life around, but he might not have been able to make that choice had there not been a number of people in his community who had helped him along the way. Not only did his school stick with Mark even though he was a really difficult kid for a long time, but also his parents finally started treating him more appropriately. Mark's environment nurtured him, and now he's a happy, active participant in that environment.

DID YOU KNOW?

According to a study by Temple University, teens behave 40-60 percent more recklessly when they think they're being watched by peers.

CHAPTER 27

Terry
The Girl Whose True Self Emerged Under Pressure

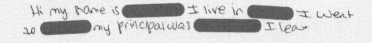

This summer I'm taking chemistry in ▮▮▮ college because I want to become a P.A. iyh, but it turns out the class is much harder than I expected and I'm studying everyday and stressed out! So I'm still deciding if I'm gonna take chem 2 second half but if not, I can finally have a summer!

Hi my name is ▮▮▮ I live in ▮▮▮ I went to ▮▮▮ my principal was ▮▮▮ I lea~

Indicator	Meaning
Rigid/controlled writing	Fear of losing control
Some of the lines move upward	Hiding sadness with "good girl" image
Words are close together	Likes to connect with others
Wavy lines across page	Insecurity
Small lower zone	Emotional insecurity, lacking vocabulary for her emotions, needs outside approval

Last two (quickly written) lines are fluid, fast, and flexible	Works better under pressure
Personal pronoun I shows pressure from the upper line	Clash with mother

Analysis: Putting It Together

Terry's handwriting cries out, "I lost control once, and I don't want to lose it again." (What exactly happened is unclear.) By making a lot of rules for herself and others, she maintains an illusion of safety, power, and control. Unfortunately, that illusion is often just that—an illusion. Beneath a bright, "good girl" image that she works very hard to maintain, Terry hides sadness.

Terry is a connector, meaning she likes to be around people and gains energy from her relationships. She's a great conversationalist; she can make good conversation out of almost anything. This personality trait comes with a downside: She cares too much about what other people think and want, which makes her confused about her own true goals and her own true self.

For example, Terry's mother has high expectations for Terry. Terry is a connecter and a people-pleaser, so she tries to please her mother at almost any cost, but it puts too much pressure on Terry, causing her to become resentful and defensive. She needs to create a certain amount of emotional distance from her mother's expectations in order to have a healthy relationship with her mother and with herself. This is true of all others' expectations. That's not to say that her mother's expectations don't matter, just that she shouldn't base her entire self-worth and identity on them.

Interestingly, a lot of these issues seem to lessen or disappear when Terry is under stress. Stress makes her temporarily forget her need for control, power, and defense mechanisms, and her natural fluidity, intelligence, and joyful personality can shine. When she has to focus on an immediate task at hand, she stops thinking about protecting herself and starts being real. It's amazing how, though counterintuitive, when people give up the need for control, they reveal their true power within. Terry will thrive if she can invest in her own self-respect, minimize her expectations of others, and be motivated by her *own* potential.

DID YOU KNOW?

So many parents are insecure about their relationships with their teens, but 81 percent have a positive opinion of their fathers, and 84 percent have a positive opinion of their mothers. Additionally, more than three out of four teens enjoy spending time with their parents.

CHAPTER 28

Allen
The Bullied Boy
Who Got In His Own Way

There once was a man who had a lot of money, so much that he was able to give charity to anyone who asked. But he had one thing that made him more happy then money: he had many children, all whom set great examples. They weren't all that smart, but they were honest & all loved each other. They were a joy to be around, & gave their father much nachas.

Indicator	Meaning
Edge-to-edge writing	Doesn't want help from adults
Wavy lines across page	Insecurity
No upper margin	Quietness, difficulty opening up to others
Heavy pressure	Defensiveness
River	Keeps people far for fear of being criticized, hears opinions as criticisms
Blob	Hiding imperfections, worries what others think of him
Narrow M's and N's	Difficulty opening up to others
Retracing	Mistrust of others

Analysis: Putting It Together

Allen, age 17, is a quiet, insecure, defensive person who's addicted to protecting himself after being bullied by classmates when he was younger. Constantly on guard for anyone who *might* be dangerous, he watches and studies people, always erring on the side of caution and assuming everyone is against him. He fears opening up to others and puts *a lot* of energy trying to making sure no one can hurt him. He worries about what others will say to him, hearing opinions as facts and criticisms. He will do whatever he can to hide his imperfections.

Allen doesn't realize that he's created a problem that's blocking him from succeeding socially. He believes the bullies were right, and he underestimates himself and everyone around him. Not only has he closed himself off from listening to or being helped by anyone, but also, nobody even has the opportunity to really know the true Allen because he puts up such a strong front out of fear of being hurt. All the energy he invests in his fear makes him socially awkward and uncomfortable to be around.

Allen was surprised to hear that he was the problem in his own growth, that his fear of others became a self-fulfilling prophecy. Allen's mistreatment of himself laid the groundwork for others to mistreat him, or at the very least to be uncomfortable around him. Allen thought he was being proactive, when really he was being self-destructive. For Allen, the realization that he'd been setting himself up for failure was a major "oh my gosh!" moment. It was fascinating to watch this revelation unfold.

Our session quickly and precisely brought information to the conscious level, but the majority of the work comes after that. It's now up to Allen to work on the concepts and internalize them. If Allen can learn to focus on what's real instead of what's in his head, he'll free his mind to deal with life's unexpected changes, challenges, and chaos in the most efficient manner possible. He will feel free, and he will be happy.

My name is MG. I have been a student at a lot of schools. This is the first school where there was a handwriting expert to help students on a personal level.

Our official handwriting analysis expert is Mr. Rosenthal. He analysed my handwriting and let me know my positive and negative personality traits.

The negative trait he pointed out in me was how I could not interact with people because I had put a "wall" in front of me. I presumed I was higher than everyone else. I also used to think how no one could understand my way of thinking because I was on a higher level and not understandable by anyone.

I took his knowledgeable advice to my heart and slowly started to break the wall between me and society.

Later in my life, I noticed a huge positive change in how I treated people and how people treated me.

I believe with full faith that the advice and guidance that Mr. Rosenthal gave me changed my life for the good.

I will forever be amazed how he can help people just by analyzing their handwriting!

MG, age 18

Conclusion

THE FOLLOWING EMAIL[9] was forwarded to me a while back by the principle of a high school whose students I often mentor. Note how unbelievably understanding, open minded, and full of real love this principle is for this new student (who, by the way, she barely even knows). Can you imagine how different our teens—our *world*—would be, if every educator and parent saw their teens with such potential, acknowledged their struggles as real and legitimate, didn't view their teens' challenges as burdens, and offered them a world of opportunity with no judgement?

From: **Dena Gorkin** <DenaGorkin@bnoschomesh.com>

Subject: **New Student....yup**

Dear Super-flexible Staff,

Today we unexpectedly received a gift: a new student!

(Actually this was in the works for well over a month, but it suddenly came to fruition today.)

Alexandra Black is an 11th grader. Her parents live in Connecticut. She started off this year at a different school, but it was not a good fit. Her mother was hesitant to send her to NY because she needs a place to board, but now that is being worked out.

---

9   Some details have been changed to protect privacy.

She is a bright, capable student and is struggling to find her identity. She looks sad, but I think we can make her happy! She will be in all eleventh grade classes as well as Geometry, Biology, and English level 4. She will choose electives tomorrow or Wednesday.

Like all our students, Alexandra needs a lot of warmth and a chance to succeed. Please let us know if there is anything you see that could be of help to us in getting to know her better and fill her needs.

Thanks!

Mrs. Dena Gorkin
Principal

Our job as adults is to understand, guide, respect, and listen to our teens. We cannot control whether our teens succeed, or experience happiness, or live the lives we want for them. We cannot know what the future holds.

But there is so much we *can* do. When teens need outside help, get it for them. When they need time to figure something out, give it to them. When they do something poorly, educate them. When they think they know everything, do not feel intimidated. Be grateful; they're trying to think. When they want to be with their peers more than with you, they are normal. When their expression of life is more intense than yours, they are normal. Teenagers respond best in a safe, calm environment that's respectful, consistent, and fair.

Understanding lasts forever. We need to just be there for our teens. We don't need to change them.

I'm Me

I'm me.

The best me I can be.

No bigger

No smaller

I'm just me.

G-d made me right

To feel this might

All day and all night

I'm proud to be me.

—By Yaakov Rosenthal

About the Author

YAAKOV ROSENTHAL is a certified graphologist, trauma therapist, and life coach, as well as a holistic healer and certified physiognomist (face reader). He uses these skills during consultations with clients of all ages and backgrounds, especially in high schools and summer camps, where he coaches hundreds of teenagers annually.

Originally from Albany, New York, Yaakov completed his BA in psychology at Hofstra University. He later received accreditation from the Manhattan School of Graphology, where he was mentored by the late Felix Klein, one of the world's most renowned authorities on the subject. Since the beginning of Yaakov's graphology practice in 1992, he has shared his skill with psychologists, guidance counselors, social workers, lawyers, dating services, and Fortune 500 companies. He has given hundreds of lectures on four continents. His first book, *Unlock: The Secret World of Teenagers,* was published in 2014.

Yaakov travels around the country visiting schools as a life coach and consultant and is currently the resident mentor at three high schools in Brooklyn, New York, where he resided for 30-plus years with his wife and family. Yaakov and his wife now live in Pomona, New York.

Email yyrosenthal@gmail.com or visit understandyourteenager.com to contact Yaakov about coaching, speaking engagements, trauma therapy, etc.

Frequently Asked Questions About Graphology

Q: Where is graphology used?

A: It's used extensively in all kinds of business organizations and especially for hiring, from CEOs to truck drivers. It's used by psychotherapists and counselors in psychological diagnostic tests, as well as in personality profiles and compatibility tests. It's often used in investigations and with lie detection. Many use it as a self-help tool for individuals seeking change in their lives. I even once found the stalker of a twelve-year-old girl from his ransom note. Really, the possibilities are endless.

Q: What does it mean if my handwriting is really messy?

A: I get this question probably more than any other, I think partly because when we were younger we were drilled to write neatly. I think that is a carryover from 50 years ago before they allowed typewritten papers. The 12th grade history teacher would get 60-80 handwritten papers, and the second grade teacher was trying to help out the history teacher by having the kids write neatly. Basically, messy handwriting only means that the person has trouble verbally communicating. But even that has variations on the theme. A person with messy handwriting could be an imbecile or a genius. Depends what else is going on in the handwriting. It's only one of 22 indicators I look at.

Q: Why does my handwriting change from day to day, or minute to minute?

A: Certain characteristics in a person's handwriting can change depending on the person's mood, or on how fast he needs to write in that moment. Also, as we grow and change, our handwriting adjusts to that new maturity, or lack thereof. Teens and their handwriting change faster than older people because they're still figuring out who they are, and they are experiencing major physical changes, as well. They haven't established ingrained habits yet. I'll often take a writing sample from a teen in September, and in May we'll talk about their change—their successes and their new challenges. Some teens request it during the year: "I think I've changed, I want to see if you can pick it up." I can pick it up. The specific change can definitely be seen.

Q: Can you change your personality by changing your handwriting?

A: It's a big discussion in the industry. Some say yes, some say no. One of my colleagues developed angle-curve exercises that help you control the pen better and create a stronger hand-brain connection. Handwriting does change after those exercises, but does it change the person? I believe it depends, that it's usually a gestalt—once you're working on yourself, working on your handwriting might help. That being said, there are two things that, if I see them in a client's handwriting, I do request that he change. The first is the personal pronoun I (the way a person writes the letter I when referring to himself, as in, "I went to the store"). If the client knows the rule that the personal pronoun I is always capitalized and he doesn't do it, I request that he do it, being that a lowercase I usually indicates a feeling of inferiority/insecurity. The second thing I sometimes request he change is his signature. The signature represents what a person wants to project to the outside world. Some people will cross out their name as part of the way they sign their signature, which indicates some level of self-sabotage. I ask these people to find a new signature.

Q: Will two graphologists say the same thing about the same handwriting sample?

A: Usually. Each graphologist has his own specialty and perspective, so you will likely get some variation, but the main ideas will almost always be the same.

Q: Can graphology be explained scientifically?

A: Neuroscientists have proven that personality characteristics correlate to specific neurological brain patterns, which result in specific kinds of movements in the body. Graphologists basically interpret the personality traits that correlate to the movements made on paper as dictated by a person's neurological brain patterns.

Q: How accurate is it?

A: Graphology as a science is very accurate, like a mathematical equation, but the accuracy and depth of any individual reading will depend on the graphologist.

Q: Can graphology tell anything about the future?

A: No!

Q: What if I feel certain a graphologist analyzed something incorrectly?

A: Humans make mistakes. It's possible to misinterpret what the eyes are seeing. However, many times the person whose handwriting is being read is just not in touch and doesn't want to believe what's true. For example, I did a reading for a man whose sample indicated to me that his parents were very dominant, and that he had a hard time feeling independent from them. He responded, "I can't relate to that. It's not true." I felt pretty confident I was right, but I wasn't going to beat a dead horse. At a later point, his wife joined us, and the man asked me to repeat what I'd said about his parents. This time, he said, "You know, it actually *might* be true," to which his wife responded in a knee-jerk reaction, "You're darn tootin' it's true!"

Q: Can a writer intentionally fool a graphologist?

A: Sure, but what's the point of that? Who has anything to gain? For example, if the person gives the wrong age. I was once given a sample where the woman told me she was 25, but really she was 55. The reading of the sample dramatically changed based on the age. At 25, her sample would have been read as indicating that she had a lot of psychological problems, but at 55 the same sample indicated that she was just really eccentric. Then there are people who try to write really neatly, though this usually falls apart after a few lines. There *are* sometimes those people who work really hard to fool me. Sometimes it just looks like an obviously fake handwriting. Sometimes they really do fool me, which, in and of itself, says a lot about their personality.

Q: Does it matter what language I write in?

A: No. I have analyzed handwriting samples from people writing in English, Spanish, Portuguese, and French. I will note that, interestingly, you can see overarching national mental and emotional tendencies varying by country in the national trends in handwriting.

Q: How old is graphology?

A: The earliest known example of interpreting a person's personality from his handwriting dates back to Confucius in the year 500 BCE. He issued a warning: "Beware of a man whose writing sways like a reed in the wind." The first known publication on the study of handwriting was printed in 1622 by Italian doctor Camillo Baldi: *How To Recognize from a Letter the Nature and Quality of a Writer.* The term "graphology" was coined in 1875 by French abbot Jean Hyppolyte Michon, from the Greek "graph" (to write) and "logos" (theory).

22 Indicators Used
To Analyze Handwriting

1. Space: between letters, words, and lines

2. Margins: top, bottom, left, and right

3. Baseline: where the letters rest on the line that runs across the page

4. Zones: upper (tops of letters like H, B, and F), middle (where all letters reside), and lower (bottoms of letters like Y, G, and P)

5. Size of the letters

6. Rhythm: the ebb and flow of the writing

7. Pressure: the force used to write

8. Speed of writing

9. Whether the person writes in print, script, or print-script

10. Connective forms: whether forms are connected by angles or loops

11. Slant direction of letters

12. Line pitch: straightness of the full line of text

13. Fullness or leanness of letters: width or narrowness

14. Cover strokes: retracing portions of letters

15. Initial and terminal strokes of the letter

16. Regularity: fluidity/rigidity of letters

17. Capital letters

18. The capital letter I

19. Signature

20. Letter formations

21. Rivers: when the spaces between words align vertically up and down the page to create one long contiguous space

22. Excessive cross-outs

Acknowledgements

I AM FORTUNATE AND GRATEFUL that Mrs. Shana Balkin collaborated in the writing of my book. Her thoughtfulness, curiosity, willingness to learn, and professionalism are of the highest order. She preserved my voice and made the book flow. She also assumed the roles of literary advisor and writer. Shana's pursuit of excellence and desire to accurately express my life's work are unsurpassed. Thank you, Shana, for all your effort.

Thank you to Rabbi Moshe Lieblich, Rabbi Uri Perlman, Rabbi Menachem Blau, and Mrs. Dina Gorkin, who have challenged me, guided me, and stood by me all these years.

Much appreciation to Dan Siegel, who inspired me to explore adolescent neuroscience.

I am very grateful to Mordechai Balkin, whose superb proofreading and critical editing lended even more clarity and accuracy to the content than I could have asked for or expected.

My beta readers, Rabbi Issur Weissberg, Mrs. Chana Weissberg, Mrs. Ani Lipitz, and Dr. Regalena Melrose, collectively helped to improve the book with their invaluable feedback. Thank you.

Thank you to Tom Matkovic for the book layout and Peter O'Rourke for the cover design, both of which are artfully and professionally done.

Last but certainly not least, infinite thanks to all the beautiful teenagers I have met along the journey. You've taught me so much about life and how beautiful, precious, and fragile it is.

Sources

"Adolescent Angst: 5 Facts about the Teen Brain." Www.livescience. com/21461-teen-brain-adolescence-facts.html.

Aron, Elaine. *The Highly Sensitive Person*. New York: Harmony Books, 2016.

Bloom, Paul. *Against Empathy*. New York: HarperCollins Publishers, 2016.

"Chicago: Black Cohosh." Www.exercise.com, November 08, 2018.

DeWitt, David J. *Bullying*. Www.outshirtpress.com, 2017.

Doidge, Norman, M.D. *The Brain That Changes Itself*. London: Penguin Books Ltd., 2007.

Duckworth, Angela. *Grit*. New York: Schieber and Design, 2016.

Ford, Debbie. *The Secret of the Shadow*. New York: HarperCollins Publishers, 2002.

Forward, Susan. *Emotional Blackmail*. New York: HarperCollins Publishers, 1998.

Freeman, Tzvi. *Bringing Heaven Down to Earth*. Berkley, California: Class One Press, 1997.

Goleman, Daniel. *Emotional Intelligence*. New York: Bantam Books, 1995.

Hodakov, Rabbi Chaim Mordechai Isaac. *The Educator's Handbook*. New York: Merkos L'Inyonei Chinuch, 1998.

"It Takes A Community To Help An Adolescent": *Handbook of Community-Based Clinical Practice*.

Katie, Byron. *A Friendly Universe*. New York: Penguin Group, 2013.

Katie, Byron. *Loving What Is*. New York: Harmony Books, 2002.

Klein, Felix. *Gestalt Graphology*. New York: Universe, Inc., 2007.

Jensen, M.D. *The Teenage Brain*. New York: HarperCollins Publishers, 2015.

Kahneman, Daniel. *Thinking, Fast and Slow*. New York: Farrar, Straus, and Giroux, 2011.

Kalmenson, Mendel. *Seeds of Wisdom*. New York: Jewish Educational Media, 2014.

"Letting Go of What 'Should Be' Sl—Knitting Paradise." Www.knittingparadise.com/t-480018-1.html.

Levine, Peter. *In An Unspoken Voice*. Berkeley, California: North Atlantic Books, 2010.

Levine, Peter. *Waking The Tiger: Healing Trauma*. Berkeley, California: North Atlantic Books, 1997.

Lowe, Sheila. *The Complete Idiot's Guide to Handwriting Analysis*. Indianapolis, Indiana: Alpha Books, 2007.

"Most Teens Admire Their Parents and Enjoy Spending Time with Them: Really!" Www.childtrends.org/news-release/most-teens-admire-their-parents-and-enjoy-spending-time-with-them-really.

"Marc and Angel Hack Life – Practical Tips for Productive...." Www.marcandangel.com/page/8/.

Melrose, Regalena, Ph.D. *The 60 Seconds Fix*. Long Beach, California: 60 Second Press, 2013.

Melrose, Regalena, Ph.D. *Why Students Underachieve*. Maryland Rowman & Littlefield Publishers, 2006.

Pelcovitz, David, Ph.D., and Mandel, David. *Breaking The Silence*. Jersey City, New Jersey: Ktav Publishing House, 2011.

Rabbi Shneur Zalman of Liadi (Baal HaTanya). *Tanya*. New York: Kehot Publication Society.

Rabbi Shneur Zalman of Liadi (Baal HaTanya). *Torah Or.* New York: Kehot Publication Society, 1984.

Roman, Klara G. *Handwriting: a Key to Personality.* New York: Pantheon Books, 1952.

Schneerson, Rabbi Menachem Mendel. *Simcha: Breaking Through Barriers.* New York: Sichos in English, 2010.

Seifer, Marc, Ph.D. *The Definitive Book of Handwriting Analysis.* Franklin Lakes, New Jersey: New Page Books, 2009.

Siegel, Daniel J, M.D. *Brainstorm.* New York: Penguin Group, 2013.

"Starfish Story." Cityyear.org.

Sternberg, Laurence. *Age of Opportunity.* New York: Houghton Mifflin Harcourt Publishing Company, 2015.

Sullivan, Dan. *The 80% Approach.* Toronto: The Strategic Coach, Inc., 2013.

"Survey: 70% of Teens Hide Online Behavior from Parents." Www.cnn.com/2012/06/25/tech/web/mcafee-teen-online-survey/index.html.

"Teens Spend Nearly Nine Hours Every Day Consuming Media." Www.washingtonpost.com/news/the-switch/wp/2015/11/03/teens-spend-nearly-nine-hours-every-day-consuming-media/?utm_term=.ce8507cfbce5.

"The Most Toxic Behavior That Drains Your Mental Energy...," Www.steemit.com.

"What Teens Wish Their Parents Understood." Www.njfamily.com.

YAAKOV ROSENTHAL

Unlock: The Secret World of Teenagers

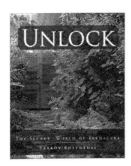

WANT TO TRY your hand at graphology? *Unlock: The Secret World of Teenagers* is a great place to start. Introductory tools and tips give you and your teen invaluable insight into your teen's inner workings, along with a broader and deeper perspective. *Unlock* lends clarity to the complexity of the teenage experience, while fostering empathy and more effective and compassionate teaching and parenting.

"I am thrilled that Yaakov Rosenthal has decided to share his gift with the world in the form of this book. It is my fervent hope that with Mr. Rosenthal's guidance, parents, educators, and youth directors of all kinds will be able to improve their understanding of the children and teens in their care. With greater understanding, we can usher the adults of tomorrow into adulthood with more self-awareness, more confidence, and greater ability to be productive members of our society."

—Dena Gorkin

Available at understandyourteenager.com and amazon.com.

Made in the USA
Middletown, DE
28 June 2019